F. DANIEL FROST
and the Rise of the Modern American Law Firm

F. DANIEL FROST

and the Rise of the Modern
American Law Firm

TONI M. MASSARO

The University of Arizona / Tucson

The University of Arizona
© 2011 The Arizona Board of Regents
All rights reserved

Produced for the University of Arizona
by Whitewing Press, Tucson, AZ 85728-5539
ISBN 978-1-888965-11-7
Library of Congress Control Number 2010939451

Manufactured in the United States of America on acid-free,
archival-quality paper containing a minimum of 30% post-
consumer waste and processed chlorine free.

16   15   14   13   12   11   6   5   4   3   2   1

Distributed by the University of Arizona Press
www.uapress.arizona.edu

Frost is simply well disposed toward life:
He loves to do right things, and to do
lots of them.

— Dr. Peter Bing

CONTENTS

✦ ✦ ✦

A photo album follows page 80.

PREFACE

✦ ✦ ✦

This is a biography of F. Daniel Frost, whose life and work are most closely associated with the national and international expansion of the Los Angeles law firm of Gibson, Dunn & Crutcher from the 1960s through the 1980s. This also is a tale of the transformation of the American legal profession, especially in the state of California, during the late twentieth century. Macrohistories offer one important window into this rich chapter of the American legal profession's history. Personal narratives of the most ambitious and high-profile leaders offer still another. This history is written from Frost's viewpoint as an exceptionally influential private lawyer who shaped a major California firm throughout the second half of the last century.

In the mosaic of the American legal profession's metamorphosis during this dynamic era, the rise of California's law firms was a crucial component. Gibson, Dunn & Crutcher today is a global entity with offices and influence in every major economic hub in the world, and it is on the leading edge of professional innovation. Yet when Frost joined the firm it still was a small, essentially regional institution. Frost was a witness to, and became a central architect of, the firm's dramatic evolution thereafter. He had a bird's-eye view of the many forces that altered the face of the legal profession.

Frost began at the first rung of associates, ascended to partner in 1956, became a senior partner and part of the management team in 1962, and was elected as the first chairman of the Management Committee in 1979. As chair, he led the firm through a period of staggering growth. He retired as an active partner in 1988, and he remains to this day in intermittent communication with the firm's leadership.[1]

When Frost began as an associate with Gibson, Dunn & Crutcher, the national population of lawyers was barely 220,000. When he later began his stint as one of the firm's managers, the law firm had only sixty-four lawyers and a gross annual income of $3.8 million. By April of 1986, however, the firm had grown to nearly 530 lawyers, with twelve offices in the United States and abroad, and a gross annual income of more than $156.2 million. When he left active practice a few years later, the firm had reached a stunning $236.9 million in revenue, and had more than 650 lawyers.

Like all of the most successful law firms of this era, Gibson Dunn's identity from its founding in 1890 throughout most of the twentieth century was aligned closely with the personalities of a few powerful individuals. At Gibson Dunn, one of the strongest of these personalities was Frost's.

As manager, Frost governed with steely resolve, an almost uncanny ability to anticipate the future, and relatively few collaborators—despite the firm's philosophy that its leaders were "first among equals." His success as a leader derived from a combination of life experiences, the law firm's sound structure and growth opportunities, and favorable external socioeconomic forces.

Born to a moderately well-to-do California stockbroker and his wife, Frost was a true California son. He was educated outside the elite East Coast training ground of the hidebound "white shoe" law firms of the mid-twentieth century and came from pioneer stock. He rose to the very top leadership post of one of the nation's most respected firms at a moment when American law firms generally were undergoing tectonic shifts of unmatched force. By all accounts, he negotiated his firm imaginatively and successfully for more than a quarter century, through tumultuous changes in the demographics, management, economics, practice environments, and professional identities of American law firms. He eventually steered the firm into a national and international leadership position among the most powerful firms in the nation. Most remarkably, he maintained the firm's character and collegiality despite the centrifugal forces of the times.

The foundation of Frost's success had two primary pillars. The first pillar was Frost's family, his education, and his public service background—including thirty-nine months in the China-Burma-India (CBI) theater during World War II. In these personal experiences lay the seeds of a lawyer-to-be who possessed both the desire and the capacity to navigate the choppy waters of the 1960s through the 1980s and one who saw the global possibilities of practice at a young age.

The second pillar was the historical and economic context in which Frost lived. Context and opportunity matter much in a professional life, and both worked to Frost's advantage. Most notably, Frost was a member of an old-line California firm that had the capacity to become a major national force, in a professional environment that increasingly rewarded the strong and vanquished weaker entities. Although only a western firm in 1951, Gibson Dunn had the potential to become a national force when major American law firms began their era of expansion: it had a reputation for excellence in its realm and had the right fundamentals.

It also had a tremendous geographical advantage. During the second part of the last century, California's major industries, leading universities, cultural centers, and sheer geographical expanse and natural beauty established the state as the nation's *other* coast—rivaling, and in some respects defeating, the venerable East Coast in influence, affluence, and dynamism. "Go west, young man" became an adage for many twentieth-century entrepreneurs and profession-als—no less than it was for many nineteenth-century pioneers—because emerging technologies, creative investors, and ambitious innovators gravitated toward California's golden economic opportu-nities, its academic hubs, and its intellectual and cultural riches.

Of course, such contextual opportunities are only chances to succeed. Knowing how and when to act upon them involves a mys-terious medley of human qualities, including the capacity to appre-hend possibilities and to make the most of the times in which one lives. Frost possessed these elusive qualities and had the drive to carry himself and his firm to the forefront of the emerging "big firm" era of the American legal profession. His strategies were both prescient and profoundly practical.

This biography analyzes the main elements of Frost's strategy, especially his growth philosophy and financial tactics. He recognized early on that expansion was a necessary predicate to the enduring influence and profitability of the firm. Each new office, he believed, had to benefit the whole, and each had to share a common com-mitment to preserving a unitary sense of firm culture. Frost rejected use of the term "branch" for new offices, because he thought it was derogatory. Several major East Coast firms had used that term when starting a presence in Southern California and failed to incorporate the California lawyers into their culture, management, and pool of profits. Frost felt this was sure to cause—and indeed it did cause—serious rifts and, in some cases, eventual dissolution of the arrange-ment. Frost was determined to have every Gibson, Dunn & Crutcher office consider itself an integral part of the whole, with a partner in charge who was incorporated into regular meetings with the firm's senior management and the other partners. This turned out to be an important feature of the success of the firm's expansion.

Frost also saw—in a non-dewy-eyed way—that a modern law firm's success depended upon its relative profitability. Modern lawyers' desire for financial success had become an ever more powerful motivator when they chose their law firms and practice settings. No longer was a loftier sense of law as a noble calling the exclusive touchstone for many professionals. Frost therefore sought to advance both needs—profits and professionalism—within the larger context of providing clients with the best possible legal representation in order to maintain the firm's competitive edge. At every turn, he appealed to his colleagues' higher angels—by stressing the common character of the firm and its culture of collegiality—but he never romanticized the lawyers or the profession as a whole. Frost accepted that business imperatives make or break a law firm, no less than any other economic concern, and based policies on a pragmatic sense of how people and businesses actually function. In this respect, he anticipated and was prepared for the most fundamental change in law firm philosophy of his generation: the shift away from viewing law as a "profession," in a nineteenth-century sense, to seeing it as a complex business conducted by legal professionals, in a late twentieth-century sense.

The chronicle ends with a glance at Frost's life beyond his time at the firm. Where does a business leader, still at the prime of his life and in excellent health, direct his energy and insights after decades of being in charge of a global entity such as Gibson, Dunn & Crutcher? In Frost's case, the answer was twofold: he pursued new business ventures, and he devoted himself to worthy philanthropies. Here, too, Frost's early influences informed his choices about the businesses, the institutions, and the people to which and to whom he devoted his attention and resources.

Frost's career holds valuable lessons for historians of the legal profession, for California historians, and for lawyers of any era. In particular, it offers insights into the management of large, private law firms and into how an individual lawyer can become influential in his or her respective professional realm.

Frost's life also offers insights for his professional and personal descendants. As a leader, Frost respected and sought to preserve the firm's history. He recognized that the lawyers of his generation were deeply indebted to the ones who predated them and was careful to recognize this debt. He also became a student of history of the American West and spent many years capturing the history of his pioneer ancestors. In both arenas—professional and personal—he sought to create an accurate and nuanced account of others' lives in order to protect their legacy and to locate modern events and people in their historical contexts. Yet Frost's own story often was muted in his retelling of others' lives, because his emphasis was on the firm as a team, and on his pioneer family as a mosaic. Implicitly, of course, Frost himself was, in many ways, the cord that bound all of these narratives together.

This account is told expressly from Frost's perspective, and it is aimed at illuminating his individual role in the evolving firm and family history. It amplifies these other histories, and may enable Frost's professional and personal descendants to find themselves in an ongoing evolution of a pioneer law firm and a pioneer family as they extend across generations, landscapes, and time. Frost's heirs in particular may glimpse their own trajectory, as they reflect on the life of this western lawyer, professional leader, entrepreneur, and philanthropist—a journey that continues as of this writing.

Acknowledgments

Thanks are owed to many people who provided valuable input to this project. First and foremost is Dan Frost himself, who spent countless hours sharing his rich life story with me. This account is drawn from his vivid and detailed memories of the many people and events described herein.

Thanks also go to Sue Frost, Ken Doran, Ron Beard, William Wegner, Dr. Peter Bing, and Russ Burtner for their input, and to the lawyers of Gibson, Dunn & Crutcher—especially Nancy P. McClelland—who conducted extensive oral interviews with Frost in 1984, 1985, 2004, and 2005 that were invaluable resources.

Sonya Manes did a superb job as copyeditor and improved the manuscript in every respect. Kathryn Conrad and Allyson Carter at the University of Arizona Press were the heroines of the project, by seeing its value and assuring the story was told. Harrison Shaffer of Whitewing Press gave the book its physical form and assembled a talented team of people devoted to high editorial standards.

I owe an enormous debt to Sandy Davis and Judy Parker for their work in producing and providing important feedback on the manuscript. Genevieve Leavitt helped to create the Blackburn/Frost family history, and also was—along with Sandy Davis—a sounding board and guide throughout the project. At the University of Arizona, Provost Meredith Hay and Dean Lawrence Ponoroff provided crucial support in the form of a research leave to produce the work.

Finally, I thank the alumni and friends of the University of Arizona James E. Rogers College of Law who support the mission of the college with their time and resources. This book is written about one of the college's distinguished alumni, but it is dedicated to all of them. In particular, it is dedicated to those who take seriously the obligation to pass the gift of higher education on to the generations that follow. Education is a common good—and one that requires robust public and private support. Through excellent and accessible public education, we assure that lives like Frost's can be fully lived and that the promise of future generations is fully realized.

F. DANIEL FROST

and the Rise of the Modern American Law Firm

CHAPTER ONE

✦ ✦ ✦

Western Roots

Daniel Frost is a tall, handsome man with blue-gray eyes that sparkle with interest in the world around him. He has the analytical mind and determination of an ambitious business-person and lawyer, along with the taciturn and landscape-connected spirit of a western rancher. Even in his late eighties, Frost projects the self-assured and commanding presence of someone scanning the horizon for risk, opportunity, and adventure.

Frost also has a complex personality with powerful, often contradictory, instincts and aspects. He is capable of great warmth and enduring friendships, but can appraise a business deal with cold precision and can plot strategy without a trace of sentimentality. He laughs easily—at the world and himself—and has a marvelous ability to enjoy his physical surroundings and to appreciate the moment. Yet he does not—as the expression goes—"suffer fools lightly," and wastes neither time nor money. Once he sets a course, he commits himself wholly to the endeavor, no matter what obstacles emerge; he is relentless in pursuit of a goal.

Professionally, he is quite transparent—in the sense of letting others see his intentions clearly in his business and other public dealings. Personally, he can be opaque, in the sense of keeping his motivations close to the vest and guarding well his privacy. A devout Catholic, he believes in a force greater than man or nature. He nevertheless refuses to allow his fate to be determined wholly by circumstances or chance; rather, he seeks to dictate outcomes.

The roots of Frost's complexities extend back into his family history. His character was influenced by his American western background, which reaches to the pre–Civil War era on both his paternal and maternal sides. He has written that "I have buried deeply in my genes a love of the West, vast open spaces, and cattle and horses." Yet this "range-free" aspect of his self-concept—of his soul, in fact—is perpetually in creative tension with his cosmopolitan instincts and with the fact that many professional opportunities can only be found in a major metropolis. His lifelong effort to manage these paradoxical draws is best captured by one illustration: Frost soothed his "country spirit" by placing a worn leather saddle in the trunk of his automobile when he drove into Los Angeles to the gleaming high-rise that, still, houses the Gibson, Dunn & Crutcher law firm offices. The outward appearance was of a sleek city lawyer. Beneath the surface, the saddle symbolized a longing for, and connection to, another life altogether.

The Frost rancher roots track back on both sides to western pioneers. Frost inherited a love of the land from his maternal grandfather—Nevadan Thomas Brinley Rickey—who was a prominent figure in the development of the Nevada frontier. Rickey was an early rancher whose large-scale ranching management included thousands of Nevada acres. Frost has written the following summary of his colorful grandfather:

As a teenager Rickey struck out on his own, leaving the rest of his family in the Ione, California, area near Sacramento and Sutter's Creek. (His father and uncle had established a stage coach transportation system of materials and food from Sacramento to the gold mines, and established stage coach stops along the way.) He crossed the Sierra Nevadas in the early 1850s by himself with a horse and pack mule, eventually arriving in what is now called the Carson Valley, Nevada. Nevada was not yet a state, but rather was a part of the Utah Territory. The local Indians were Paiutes, given to occasional uprisings. Rickey staked out a homestead in the most fertile part of this valley and started a cattle operation. (The exact spot is now marked by a monument erected by E Clampus Vitus, an organization dedicated to marking historic spots.) Over the years Rickey became the largest cattle rancher in the area, owning virtually all of what was then called Long Valley, and extending his operations south to Mono Lake and for summer grazing, west into the Sierras using federal grazing permits. Rickey was a very innovative cattle rancher. He initiated, near Carson City on his home ranch, the concept of what is now called a feedlot, where he held thousands of head of mature cattle for fattening prior to shipping them by rail from Carson City to San Francisco.

From the beginning, he understood the importance of feeding cut alfalfa, grain and field corn in the finishing process; keeping the animals quiet; and selecting an area for this operation near the railhead so that the cattle drive to the railhead would only take a few days and not diminish the weight of the cattle. He also understood modern cattle-breeding practices and at a young age separated the heifers from the young bulls as soon as they were weaned.[1] During this same period, Rickey became a state senator and was offered but declined the opportunity to represent his party in the gubernatorial races. He also was an entrepreneur and a banker who cut a deep swath in the Nevada economy in the late nineteenth-century and early twentieth-century landscape.

Frost's mother, Alice Brinley Rickey Frost, was born in 1899 when Thomas Rickey was already sixty-three. Rickey doted on his daughter, Alice, whom he regarded as a great gift in his later years. Frost recalls that his grandfather's love was returned in full by his mother, and that her first and fondest memory in life was riding in front of her father on his saddle.

Alice was raised and schooled at Rickey's home ranch near Topaz Lake. Her father taught her to ride horses, rope, brand, and drive cattle. She was a natural athlete and at an early age became an accomplished horsewoman. She loved the ranching life and spent her happiest years in Nevada.

Rickey provided a school on the ranch for his hundreds of employees, virtually all of whom were Native American or Mexican/Indian. The few teachers were Caucasians, brought in from the outside. Alice remembered being the only Caucasian child in her early school days, and her friends were children of the ranch hands. After school, she was free to ride her horse and join in ranching operations. In due course, however, Rickey began to worry that his daughter was not receiving a proper education for a young woman and sent her to boarding school at the Head School in Berkeley, California. This was a terrible blow to Alice, who preferred life on the Nevada ranch with her family and friends.

The Rickey genes not only carried this love of ranching and open spaces, but also a keen instinct for business development. Thomas Rickey was a skilled businessman with a pioneering, entrepreneurial spirit that included inventions and finance, engineering and agriculture. He introduced irrigation to Nevada out of the Truckee River and Walker Lake and was a pioneer of modern cattle-feeding technology. He experimented in massive irrigation techniques, and was an expert at large-scale range management and conservation practices. He also was a founder of the Cal-Nevada Power Company, a banker, a prominent politician, and—according to Frost—"a self-taught lawyer."[2] In these ways Frost's own spirit, with its competing allegiances—city and country, business and agriculture, a sophisticated professional life in a major national law firm and a love of horses galloping over a vast western landscape—mirrors that of his maternal grandfather.

Yet Frost's paternal relatives were no less colorful or influential on young Frost. His paternal great-grandfather, Daniel Drew Blackburn, was one of the original Anglo settlers in central California and one of the founders of Paso Robles.[3] Although born in Virginia, he spent his early childhood in what is now West Virginia, where his father died when Daniel was six. Their community consisted of small farms occupied by hardworking dirt farmers. When his father died, he left his wife to raise six children alone. Growing up under these dire circumstances, and in this location, forced the children to become serious at a very young age in order to help support their mother. This required ingenuity and tremendously hard work.

Daniel had an older brother, William, who in the early 1840s made the long, arduous journey to California and established himself in Santa Cruz. He built a sawmill there from scratch. When William wrote home of the virtues of California living, these letters led Daniel and his brothers James and Jacob to make the long, overland journey. The journey took nearly a year to complete and took the men across the Donner Pass years before the Donners.

In 1846 California was part of Mexico, then controlled by the Spanish. In that year, William Blackburn left his comfortable existence at Santa Cruz to join General John C. Frémont as a lieutenant of artillery in the Bear Flag Revolt.[4]

The Bear Flag Revolt consisted of little more than 200 volunteers who marched south from Monterey, then the capital of Alta California, or the California Territory, through the area now known as Paso Robles and San Luis Obispo. The volunteers eventually turned east to march through the Santa Ynez Valley and traversed the San Marcos Pass under a severe winter rainstorm until they arrived on the coastal plain just above Santa Barbara.

The Santa Barbara Presidio was then a Spanish fort; when the soldiers advanced on it, they found that the Spanish had fled south. The battle was finally joined just north of Los Angeles at La Cienega.[5] These troops won the encounter and ended Spanish rule.[6] After the revolt, William returned to his sawmill at Santa Cruz and served for the rest of his life as Santa Cruz's first alcalde, a combination of mayor and judge. He was an earthy and humorous judge—a "Will Rogers" type—according to accounts in the Bancroft history of the area.[7]

In 1857, Daniel Blackburn, his brother James, and their partner, Lazarus Godshaux, bought the 25,993-acre Rancho Paso de Robles. There were few improvements on the ranch. One, located near what is now Templeton, was a small adobe ranch house. Again according to family lore, it was there that Margarita (Maggie) Blackburn—Frost's paternal grandmother— was born. A few years later, her father moved the family to a home he built in what is now Paso Robles.[8]

The Blackburns ran cattle and were among the original "Californios." Daniel Blackburn married late in life, and he and his young wife had fourteen children, twelve of whom survived childbirth. The sons were trained as ranchers while the daughters, including Frost's grandmother, were educated in a convent school and then married, in keeping with the expectations of the day.

Frost remembers these Blackburn relatives as classic Old World Spanish—proud, traditional, and elegant. He was told as a child that they practiced the traditions of Californios—which meant that they were exceptionally warm and generous hosts, consistent with California culture of that time. When visitors arrived at the Paso Robles hacienda-style ranch, they were greeted with open-ended hospitality; guests often stayed for days, even weeks, in the warm embrace of the Blackburn clan.

None of the Blackburn children, however, was educated for the modern world, or had strong business instincts. The next generation of Blackburns lived modestly throughout their lives—content and place-bound, but not prosperous. All retained a nineteenth-century, small-town sensibility about finances throughout their long lives. For example, when the Blackburn family real estate—the family's primary asset—eventually was passed on to the Blackburn children, it was divided into pieces and distributed among the many siblings. The heirs were not savvy about their inheritance, and the assets were quickly frittered away on automobiles and other evanescent goods, rather than invested in potentially enduring concerns. Funds were borrowed against the land from so-called Yankee bankers from San Francisco. The Blackburns lacked the income and resources to repay the loans, and they ultimately lost the land.

Maggie was the oldest of the Blackburn daughters. In 1896, she married Frost's grandfather, Francis Daniel Frost. The couple eventually moved from Paso Robles to the San Francisco Bay Area, and then farther north, just above Sacramento, where her husband tried his hand at fruit farming. To this day this is a famous area for fruit farming, but during his first few years as a farmer, Frost's operations incurred severe freezes and he lost his entire investment. This setback is believed to have contributed to his early death from a heart attack.

Frost's death left the task of raising their only child, Francis Daniel Frost Jr., to Maggie. She moved to Berkeley with her son, where their life was one of genteel poverty. Her only income was a small rent she received from inherited Paso Robles property.

Francis Daniel Frost Jr. grew up in the Berkeley area where he attended Berkeley schools and later the University of California, Berkeley. He was at heart an urban person, and never liked his early years in Paso Robles. He was better suited to city rather than country life, and once said he "hated being behind the ass of a horse." While a student at the University of California, he met Alice Brinley Rickey, whose father had moved to Berkeley to be near his daughter.

The University of California, Berkeley is a land grant college, and the male freshmen of the time were enrolled in the ROTC. Frost did well in the ROTC, and was sent to Officer Training School in early 1918. He became a second lieutenant and received orders to be shipped to Europe. He and Alice decided to be married before he left, but the Armistice occurred before he embarked and he soon received a discharge.

Upon discharge, Francis worked for his father-in-law, Thomas Rickey, who owned a farm implement business. Francis's first job was as a salesman for his father-in-law, but, as he later told his son, he was a total disaster in selling farm equipment. He felt little or no rapport with farmers, and they sensed this. In his next job as a stock-broker, Francis finally found his niche in life. He loved the business and was good at it. He and Alice began their family, and the couple had two sons and two daughters: Barbara Rickey Frost (Harkness), F. Daniel Frost, Alice Rickey Frost (Douglas/Thomas/Kennedy), and Thomas Rickey Frost.

Francis initially did quite well in the brokerage business. He was known by his peers as highly competent, ethical, and industrious. But the Great Depression slowly eroded the financial gains he had realized during the 1920s, and the decline of the family's economic fortune led to a kind of dual life for the Frost family. On the surface, and by occupation, the Frosts were very well-to-do, sophisticated, educated, and able to move comfortably in upper-middle-class social circles. Beneath the surface, the family struggled to maintain their upper-echelon lifestyle and the elite social connections to which they had become accustomed before the financial devastation of the Depression. This tension left a lasting impression on all of their children, especially Dan.

Dan saw at an early age that economies cycle, and that the good fortune of yesterday may not endure into tomorrow. He also learned that marriages often can suffer under the strains of financial worries and conflicting desires. He recalls his parents' relationship as occasionally stormy, and believes that the root of his parents' difficulties was that they had fewer resources than could sustain Alice's loftiest social aspirations. The narrative line passed on to young Frost by his father was that Frost's mother "lived beyond their means," and expected Francis to maintain the lifestyle that they had enjoyed in their early years, when his brokerage house work was thriving. Francis believed that his wife thought of herself as "an heiress who had lost her riches." This may have been so: Alice inherited nearly $175,000 from Thomas Rickey after his death in 1920, but this modest inheritance was not enough to insulate the family from the economic vicissitudes of the Depression. Yet according to Francis, Alice maintained throughout her life the expectations and the self-image of a much-adored, even pampered daughter of an older, doting father.

Francis could not live up to these expectations, though he made every attempt to maintain both the reality and the illusion of greater financial prosperity. The Frost family continued to socialize with the California upper class, and when the *Los Angeles Times* reported on Alice Rickey Frost's death in 1988, it described her as an important social figure—"a horticulturist known for nearly 60 years for her civic and philanthropic activities in Pasadena."[9] She was a founder of Pasadena Beautiful, an organization that conceived and put into effect the beautiful central landscaped parkway running the length of Lake Avenue, the main commercial street there. She became president of Descanso Gardens, the Arboretum, and the Garden Club, and later was an officer in the National Garden Club. Alice was an avid and able horticulturist and, although self-taught, was a licensed landscape designer.[10]

Behind the scenes, however, husband and wife were at odds.

Alice chided her husband for "losing her trust money," and in general for not fulfilling her life dreams. Francis, in turn, rebuked Alice for possessing illusions about her station in life, and once cruelly accused Alice's father, Thomas Rickey, of being a "jailbird." This barb, Francis knew, was an unfair one and particularly painful to his wife, who revered her father and was deeply proud of her Rickey name.

The accusation against Rickey was based on an incident in Rickey's life during the Financial Panic of 1907 when Rickey ran the State Bank & Trust Company in Nevada. Like many banks during this financial crisis, Rickey's bank did not survive the downturn. On October 22, 1907—one day before the bank closed—a bank clerk at the Goldfield branch accepted a $200 deposit. This sole event, of which Thomas Rickey had no personal knowledge (Rickey was in Carson City), led to a criminal prosecution: he was charged with fraud. In order to expedite resolution of the legal matter through the writ of habeas corpus, Rickey spent one night in jail in three different jurisdictions. The case ultimately was heard by the Nevada Supreme Court, which completely exonerated Rickey.[11] The court noted in its opinion that the "indictment does not allege an offence known to the law" under any authority.[12] Newspaper accounts of the day had covered Rickey's arrest in tabloid fashion but later made no mention of his release or judicial exoneration. This cast a libelous shadow over Rickey's name for many years, which finally was lifted when a book was written about him by Susan Imswiler many decades later.[13] Imswiler's biography underscores that the Nevada Supreme Court exonerated Rickey from any malfeasance, and maintains that the charges against Rickey were politically inspired.[14]

✦　✦　✦

All of these family stories and experiences shaped young Frost in ways that later enabled him to accomplish more in his life than he might have without these influences. For example, his parents' early prosperity, their natural intelligence, their social aspirations, and their professional and financial ambitions prompted them to guide young Frost to respect and pursue advanced education. Their social ties gave him an entrée into California business and upper-middle-class social circles; they in turn tutored him in California elite environments and provided invaluable relationships that served him well in his later years as a lawyer. When Frost entered law practice, he already knew many influential businesspeople—which included potential clients—and was known and liked by them. He also was exposed at an early age to Wall Street vernacular, which put him at ease in the business world.

His family's experiences—both witnessed and inferred from his parents' and grandparents' stories—also generated skepticism about politically driven agendas that can taint a reputation, and fostered an abiding abhorrence of debt and financial imprudence. Frost gleaned in particular from the family narratives the perils of lost financial fortunes. He was determined not to suffer a similar fate, and maintained throughout his life a wariness about financial risk and a conservatism about financially speculative ventures. He also became as talented at, and as committed to, building a solid financial foundation—for his own family and, later, for his law firm—as the Blackburns were at letting economic opportunities slip through their fingers, or—in the case of his parents—having them wrested away by a fickle economy. Frost never forgot that a life's labors and one's social and financial security can evaporate in an instant.

Yet, unlike many others scarred by the Depression, Frost was willing to take calculated risks, rather than hew solely to the security of the known. Also from the Blackburns' example, he learned that resisting the inevitable change too can lead to lost fortunes.

Finally, Frost became a person willing to assume outsized responsibilities in order to provide a better life for himself and for others—

for his family, his firm, his clients, and a range of other beneficiaries of his business acumen, his resources, and his prudence. This overwhelming sense of responsibility for others may have been driven in part by Frost's close relationship with his mother. Having seen that Alice's life dreams never were realized, Frost became the ultimate provider and caretaker for others—financially and otherwise. In short, he sought to become the breadwinner that his own father was not able to be for his wife. At the same time, he saw that his mother's expectations of his father were unrealistic, even unfair. The tension between these two realizations made Frost wary of financial failure, but also of fantasies about prosperity. He developed an uncommonly mature sense of how to build a solid future, rather than foolishly risk one's energy pursuing unattainable ends.

The result was a sophisticated and strategic person—one who understood and respected danger, but also maintained a sense of the future's promise. His father's strengths and his limitations, his mother's dreams and her disappointments, his forebearers' pioneering spirit and their lost opportunities, his country's booms and its busts—all of these elements shaped Frost. He still had a dreamer's heart—perhaps from his pioneer roots—but it was leavened by a pragmatic, sober sense of reality. This combination would prove to be a powerful one that produced exceptionally successful outcomes across multiple terrains.

✦ ✦ ✦

CHAPTER TWO

Education and Service

The twentieth century dramatically transformed the role of formal education in shaping a young person's life chances. In the early decades, relatively few Americans attended college, yet many were able to lead prosperous lives without even a high school degree. By the close of the century, however, modern professionals could not succeed without excellent and extensive educational opportunities. A college degree became a new baseline for professional success, and graduate work had become essential to professional achievement.

Frost's parents anticipated this shift and sacrificed much to assure that their children were placed in the best possible educational environments. In their son Dan's case, the quest for the right school had to be matched with his need for the right climate.

Frost suffered from serious asthma along with the limitations of pulmonary medicine of the early 1900s. His asthma was greatly aggravated by the heavy, moisture-filled air of the Bay Area, where the family lived in the 1920s. The inadequate medical options of the era—the primary treatments for serious asthma were dry air and inhalation therapies—coupled with the Bay Area's climate, ultimately proved too much for Frost's frail lungs. His father thus transferred to Los Angeles in 1929, where he headed up his company's Southern California office and hoped that the drier air would be a tonic for his ailing son.

In his Berkeley elementary school, Frost had proved himself to be a quick and early learner and therefore skipped a year. When the family moved to Southern California in 1929, this acceleration continued and he enrolled as a fourth grader in the San Marino Public School system. Believing that public school was not strict enough, his parents transferred him to Polytechnic School in Pasadena, which was located across the street from Cal Tech.[1] The curriculum was vigorous and the teachers engaging.

Frost was elected president of the student body in the ninth grade, was captain of various athletic teams, and was the top student in his class. After he graduated from Polytechnic School in 1936, he began tenth grade at South Pasadena High School. He again was a popular student and discovered the allures of girls, athletics, and a busy social life. An avid outdoorsman, young Frost also enjoyed swimming, surfing, tennis, sailing, and fly-fishing. Indeed, these nonacademic interests proved so engaging that Frost's parents soon decided that he needed fewer distractions from his studies and would benefit from a more serious, academic environment. In 1937, they enrolled their fifteen-year-old son in Phillips Academy Andover.

The Andover entrance requirements included college SATs, performance on which determined whether one was admitted and, if so, at what level. Frost was accepted and placed in the eleventh grade, called "upper middle" at Andover. But Andover turned out to be a rude awakening for this talented, even cocky, student. In the 1930s, California still was a relatively young state, lacking East Coast sophistication or pretensions. Frost had excelled easily there; in his own words he thought he was "a hotshot." Andover, in stark contrast, had been founded during the American Revolution. George Washington spoke at the school in its first year of operation, and John Hancock signed the school's articles of incorporation. This distinguished institution had long attracted the most promising students from across the nation and abroad, most of whom came from astoundingly privileged families. As Frost later said, "Andover was a *big* comeuppance—my first!"

At Andover, Frost was exposed to a world of influence and ideas previously unknown to him. He also was confronted face to face with students whose level of sophistication was stunning to a native westerner. At that time, Andover had the practice of accepting two graduates of British "public schools" and two similar exchange students from Germany. Frost was very impressed with these exchange students' educational polish, their command of world events, and their intellectual depth. Frost recalls in particular a Sunday luncheon early on in his tenure at Andover, held in the suite of the housemaster of his dormitory, Bancroft Hall. The housemaster and his wife were both English, and the two British exchange students were the other guests at the luncheon. The conversation ranged from international affairs, to monetary policy, to historical events. Frost sat in virtual silence, completely at sea. When the wife of the British housemaster turned to him and asked, "So, Mr. Frost, how do *you* feel about Ramsay McDonald?" Frost could not utter a word; he had no idea who McDonald was. Frost recalls that "it hit me right between the eyes then, that *I didn't know anything*." It was "an epiphany."

Once the housemaster's wife realized that Frost had no clue how to respond, she deftly turned the conversation away from the topic of the Labour Party prime minister. But Frost neither forgot this chastening experience nor underestimated thereafter the chasm between the salon culture of East Coast educational cosmopolitans and the more open, but still relatively unsophisticated, environment of California.

A second epiphany occurred in the Andover classroom. Frost had gone from a rigorous intellectual setting at Polytechnic in the ninth grade directly into the eleventh grade at Andover with essentially no additional studies, because his tenth grade year at South Pasadena High School was a virtual repeat of what he had learned in the ninth grade at Polytechnic. This abrupt transition and lack of preparation caused him considerable academic trauma. For example, he had done well in Latin back in California, but at Andover he was underwater. He remembers that his first interim grade in Latin was a 40—failing.

Determined to catch up, Frost began studying with far more energy and purpose than ever before, now having learned "what real studying meant." He worked extremely hard to prove himself in this rarified, demanding, and foreign atmosphere. He also made friends, and even was invited to join six of the Andover fraternities.

But just as Frost was developing academic and social traction, the Boston area was steeped in a deep fog. The winter of 1938 also brought heavy snow, which retriggered his severe asthma. The bout of illness drove him into the infirmary, where he remained for several months. By spring, his parents determined that Frost's poor health made it impossible for him to continue at Andover. They withdrew him from school and met him in New York. Together the family sailed for Europe in 1938, to pursue business matters and to explore the region.

When the family returned to the United States later that year, Frost was enrolled in the Flintridge High School for Boys in Pasadena. He completed high school there, in 1940. Once again, he made friends quickly, despite his very transient academic years. His affable personality and strong instinct for leadership positions benefited him greatly despite the frequent moves. He was chosen as student body president, and once again rose to the top of his class. It was at Flintridge that Frost took his first course in political science, which included constitutional law. He loved the material, and for the first time thought about law as a career.

The final chapter in Frost's education played out in Tucson. Frost began college in California, first attending Berkeley and then, due to poor health, Pasadena Junior College. When the severe asthma and allergies continued to dog him, Frost finally decided—like so many fellow sufferers of this era—to seek the relief of the dry air of the Sonoran Desert. On his doctor's advice, he headed to the Southwest and enrolled in the University of Arizona, Tucson.

When Frost stepped off the train in the summer of 1942, he confronted the fierce Arizona heat for the first time. He recalls the experience as akin to "walking into an oven." A neophyte's confrontation with the almost unfathomable intensity of the desert summer sun is a stunning, invariably memorable, experience. So it was with Frost.

Yet Frost not only adapted to his new Arizona home; he thrived there. During that first Tucson summer, he lived in Yavapai Hall— which, like all of the dormitories of that time, was un-air-conditioned and Spartan. He enrolled in summer school, and supported himself by doing survey work at the Tucson-based Davis-Monthan Air Force field and working at a local copper mine in Morenci, Arizona.

One then could pursue a law degree—an LLB—as an undergraduate. Frost took this opportunity, and began his law studies in 1942. The law courses triggered Frost's third epiphany: he discovered he had exceptional instinct for, and love of, analyzing cases— the standard fare of law students, both then and now. He actually *enjoyed* the grueling law school curriculum of the day.

In the 1940s, of course, admission to law school was vastly easier than surviving the law program. The attrition rate was high, lending force to the adage "Look right, look left; only one of you will remain at the end of the day." This venerable "law school-as-crucible" principle operated fully at Arizona, and the professors ruth-lessly pruned the class down to the most promising students. But Frost more than survived this process; he was elected student body president, excelled at legal studies, and laid the groundwork for his professional identity as a leader among lawyers.

In an effort to expedite his studies, Frost spent a summer session at the University of Kansas School of Law. But in 1943, World War II interrupted his education. Although Frost was eager to enlist in the armed forces, his severe asthma, as well as scar-ring from a bout of serious eye infections, rendered him "4-F," a classification that made him ineligible for active military duty. Deeply disappointed, he instead volunteered for an organization that drove ambulances and provided other support for the mili-tary. Frost eventually spent thirty-nine months overseas. As it hap-pened, his assignments and the nature of the conflict in the China-Burma-India region involved him in the war as fully as any foot soldier, and his final classification was "4-A," certifying that he had completed his military obligation.

Frost was involved with the Fourteenth Indian Army in India and Burma. His unit was attached to the Thirty-third Corps, Second Division, and sent immediately to the Fourteenth Indian Army in Assam and Burma in 1943. He later was transferred to the Eleventh East African Division, Twenty-sixth Brigade, Eleventh Battalion Headquarters Company, as part of the brigade's only medical trans-portation unit.

These times were extremely tumultuous ones for the region; for example, Frost was a witness there to some of the war's most harrow-ing and historic events. He recalls the exploits of the Indian general Bose, who defected during the war and took as many Indian sol-diers as possible with him to the Japanese army. Called Bose's Army, these Indian soldiers wore Japanese uniforms but never were fully integrated into the Japanese forces. Rather, they were relatively ill equipped, ill fed, and ill treated by the Japanese. Frost was in Burma at this time, as part of an advancing army, and saw these forces in their reduced state. Like many American soldiers of the era, young Frost viewed Bose and his followers as terrible traitors to their country. He later realized—after studying India's history and gaining a deeper appreciation of the country's internal ethnic strife and colonial history—that Bose was to many Indians a hero of the Indian independence movement.

Frost remained in the CBI theater for over three years. He first went into training with the American Field Service (AFS) at Poona (now called Pune), near Bombay (now Mumbai). He received instruction in medics and jeep ambulance mechanics, and also was given small arms training. This arms training was absolutely necessary because the Japanese army refused to honor the principle of the Geneva Convention that prevented firing upon medical corps personnel. Consequently, Frost and his cohorts in the region always bore arms, including Enfield rifles, Sten guns, and Bren automatic weapons. The Red Cross symbol that in other regions offered protection to medics was abandoned in the Far East theater, in order to better protect the medics and their patients. Officers likewise removed their rank identification to avoid targeting by the Japanese.

Each AFS jeep had two stretchers, one on top of the other. When the Japanese advanced across the Chindwin River (in Burma) toward Imphal (in India) in spring 1944, Frost and his unit were rushed into the fray, attached to the British Second Division, Fourteenth Indian Army at the famous battles of Imphal and Kohima. There, they saw heavy fighting and casualties in the so-called Forgotten War on the Assam-Burma border (Assam, part of British India and now part of independent India, was a critical strategic location for Allied forces). After Frost came down with malaria and amoebic dysentery, he ended up at a U.S. Field Hospital in Assam. He then was moved to the U.S. Army Hospital in Calcutta. When he recovered, he returned to Burma, this time with the Eleventh East African Division, which was trying to hold a blockade on the Chindwin River, a major tributary of the Irrawaddy. In Burma, Frost's unit was caught by monsoons which deluged them in more than 300 inches of rain and made it impossible for them to exit the area on the ground. Their only supplies came via air drops, and after about three months Frost finally was airlifted back to Calcutta by glider. His enlistment period up, he decided to transfer to the China National Aviation Corp. (CNAC).

The CNAC was an air service that carried military supplies over "the Hump"—the Himalaya Mountains—between Dinjan (in colonial India) and China. The CNAC's base in Shanghai lasted until 1937, when the Japanese invaded China. It then moved to Chungking (now Chongqing), where it remained until the bombing of Pearl Harbor in 1941. From 1942 to 1945, the headquarters was relocated in Calcutta.[2] In 1946 it moved back to Shanghai.

The regular route of CNAC was from the tea-producing region of Upper Assam, in the northeast province, to the Chinese air bases in Kunming. During World War II the Burma road was severed by the Japanese army, which made the treacherous flights over the Hump the only way that supplies could reach this region of China.

The CNAC provided airlifts of fuel, medical supplies, ammunition, and other supplies to U.S. and Chinese military bases in eastern China. At times CNAC would land unarmed C-47 transports at the "Flying Tiger Strip"—an island airstrip in the middle of the Yangtze River opposite the city of Chungking. These flights sometimes occurred at night to avoid Japanese fighters. Once landed at the airstrip, CNAC staff would ferry the flight crews to its hostel across from the city. At night the crews would typically be ferried across the river to the steep steps along the riverbank that led up to Chungking. Frost recalls climbing the steps and enjoying evening feasts with Chinese hosts that lasted many hours and involved rigorous drinking competitions. The Chinese—some of whom were aided by buckets barely hidden beneath the table—sought to outlast the Americans, and the festivities were "hilarious affairs" full of laughter, camaraderie, and high spirits, in every sense of the word.

Frost remained with the CNAC more than two years, stationed for most of this time in China. He made more than thirty-five trips over the Hump and, from time to time, served as a copilot for the more experienced pilots. While overseas, Frost fell in love with the region. He learned to speak some Chinese with the Chinese flight crews and, while in India, learned a little Urdu and Hindi. When on leave with CNAC, he would grab a flight back to India and, through the courtesy of U.S. and Indian air transport crews, visit the important cultural sites of India, as well as Delhi. These cultural sites included not only Agra but particularly the more remote areas such as Benares (now Varanasi), on the Ganges River, where Hindus believed bathing could cure ills and where they floated the bodies of the deceased kin in pyres in the water. He visited countless temples, where exquisite sculptures and other artwork were then unguarded and open to the public.[3]

Frost also witnessed the ethnic violence that eventually tore India asunder in 1946. Although stationed in China at the time, he visited Calcutta often and, when being driven from Dum Dum Airport (now Netaji Subhash Chandra Bose International Airport) into Calcutta, saw thousands of bodies strewn along the road. Later, he was sitting in the lobby of one of its major hotels when riots broke out there and left countless dead in their wake. His memory is of "bodies and blood everywhere."

His recollections include other momentous events aside from those he saw in India. He remembers the peace negotiations in

1946, when General Marshall attempted to negotiate an agreement between the Communists and Kuomintang in Beijing. He saw the French First Army move into Hanoi, at a time when French military archives would later deny the French were in Vietnam. He learned to pilot a C-47 and toured much of the Far East. He met Lieutenant General Claire Lee Chennault, the famed aviator who led the "Flying Tigers," and he was part of a CNAC rescue operation of a B-29 crew in Tibet. He was sent to Haiphong, Vietnam, then back to Kweilin (Guilin). He headed up the Shanghai operations at Linyong Air Field.

Frost so admired the region's peoples, cultures, music, literature, and topography that he remained in Asia for a full year after the war formally ended. After the peace treaty was signed in Tokyo Bay, ending the war in the Pacific, China remained at war within itself in the fierce struggle between the Kuomintang—led by Chiang Kai-shek—and the Communist Party—led by Mao Tse-tung. As the Russians withdrew from Manchuria, they left arms and supplies to Mao. The Kuomintang then rushed troops north of Peking (Beijing) to engage Mao, and the CNAC—the government's airfreight arm—was drafted to fly troops, arms, and equipment to supply the war in the North. This battle turned out badly for the Chiang Kai-shek government, however, and eventually led to its retreat from mainland China to the island of Formosa (Taiwan). This enormous exodus also required a huge amount of air supply, which the CNAC provided.

Frost remained in Asia until the end of 1946.[4] The time abroad instilled in him an international perspective that later gave him a global perspective on law practice long before most American professionals appreciated the importance of this outward turn in national business and professional ventures. Unlike many Americans who served in foreign wars, Frost rejected the U.S.-centered view of the world and enjoyed Far Eastern cultures. Indeed, he had hoped to return to China for professional endeavors after finishing law school, but the takeover of mainland China by the Communist Party ended that dream.

Upon his return to the states, Frost applied to Yale Law School. In the glut of postwar applicants to college and professional schools, however, the seats were filled. He thus returned to Tucson, where he completed his law studies at the University of Arizona.

By the time he resumed law school, Frost had grown as a person, citizen, and professional. He returned from the war an exceptionally motivated student who pursued his work vigorously. Among other things, he wrote an essay for the Patent Society and received the top award—$100.00—considered a princely sum at the time. The thesis of the paper was then avant-garde—that inventive business ideas should be patentable.[5]

During his law school years, Frost also began his family. He met and married Margie Miller, with whom he later had two children—Daniel Blackburn Frost, born in 1949, and Polly Frost (Sawhill), born in 1952. Law school was a happy time in Frost's life, filled with new intellectual interests and young married life.

In 1948, Frost graduated third in his law school class when the student body included future governors, future U.S. congressmen, a future U.S. secretary of the interior, and a future presidential candidate. The hardy residue of this "last-student standing" approach to legal education in the 1940s was marvelously talented, tough-minded students who were hungry for, and up to, the professional challenges ahead. Most already had been tested by the times in which they lived. Indeed, these war-era graduates remain some of the most distinguished graduates in the history of the University of Arizona College of Law's near century of graduating prominent professionals and public leaders.

✦ ✦ ✦

After graduation, Frost took and passed the Arizona bar. He left immediately thereafter for California, where he took and passed the competitive California bar. In a letter to his alma mater, Frost recorded his insights about the exam in an effort to help other Arizona law graduates prepare for this exacting exam and to encourage other students to consider California as a place to pursue their own professional goals. Frost then began his legal career, an endeavor that would consume the next four decades of his life.

✦ ✦ ✦

The Lawyering Years

The chapter of Frost's life that most defined his professional identity was his life as a practicing lawyer with Gibson, Dunn & Crutcher from 1951 to 1988. These were epochal years in the history of the legal profession, as well as for the firm, and Frost was a major player in this evolution—particularly as it unfolded in California.

During the second half of the twentieth century, the leading American private law firms morphed from regional, relatively small and close-knit institutions, into large multidisciplinary, cross-jurisdictional, and international businesses. They slowly became less defined by individual founding lawyers' personalities than by their collective identities, though these forebearers indelibly shaped the character of their firms and ushered in many of the structural changes in law firm management that, paradoxically, later rendered individual managerial personalities less salient by the close of the century.

Most young associates at elite private firms today are dimly aware—at best—of the forceful and imaginative lawyers who steered these institutions in the tumultuous environment of the 1950s through the 1980s. But their influence on the profession was truly profound. Law firm managers of the era who did not adapt to changing times watched their firms wither and die. Yet those who allowed the tempests to wholly drive their firm's agenda, without hewing to fundamental values and lessons from the past, likewise foundered. The victors in this Darwinian struggle were the few who carved a prudent path through many thickets—through minor and major recessions, the advent of legal technology, the radically changed demographics of the legal profession, the rise of lawyer advertising, the erosion of the "law firm for life" and of the "law is a jealous mistress" era of lawyer identity and loyalty to one's firm, the globalization of legal practice, the rise of the billable hour, and the emergence of law firms with 300 to 1,000 members and offices strewn across the nation and the world. All of this placed hydraulic pressures on law firm managers to find the right balance between new and old, between niche and "one-stop shopping" profiles, between metamorphosis and tradition.

Of course, every successful firm needed a sustainable strategic plan with exceptional lawyers committed to the firm's success. Yet as the American economy gathered speed after World War II, the legal profession began to adopt more of the values and practices of other businesses, along with increased competition for top lawyers. By the late 1970s, few lawyers were willing to work for the relatively modest wages of lawyers in the 1950s and '60s, and the best of them expected firms to compete for their attention and client portfolios. But leading private firms could not support their lawyers' escalating salary expectations without, in turn, requiring greater productivity from them. By the early 1990s the die was struck: firms' efforts to outbid each other in salary wars had translated into longer work hours for lawyers and tremendous pressure to elevate their billable hours.

The late 1970s also ushered in the erosion of loyalty between lawyer and firm. The firm/lawyer relationship no longer was a so-called marriage—it was a business association. Lawyers were more willing to relocate their practice when they received more lucrative offers across the street, or even across the country. This increased competition was fostered by heightened awareness of what other firms were paying. The creation of lawyer publications such as the *National Law Journal* in 1978, and the *American Lawyer* in 1979, along with their rankings of firms in terms of profits and pay, produced transparency of lawyer compensation and benefits in ways that revolutionized the profession.

The growth in American business prosperity after World War II also provided incentives for some managers to rethink conventional principles of law office management, attorney compensation, partnership tiers, and other practices. Competition for business, for lawyers, and for recognition became openly bare-knuckle—rendering the practice of law, in many lawyers' eyes, vastly less collegial.

Managers of firms, of course, could not ignore these forces, despite the potential cost to collegiality or esprit de corps. Even brand-new lawyers—though unable to sustain their pay, or even to perform much useable work without close supervision and mentoring—had begun to fetch more than $30,000 in starting salaries, not including benefits or overhead, a figure that would spiral steadily upward for decades. The most desirable of such candidates—those graduating at the top of their class in the elite law schools or exiting clerkships with the Supreme Court of the United States—were offered lucrative additional perks by firms vying for the cachet of hiring from the uppermost cadre. The arms race for talent and prestige in the high altitudes became staggering, and firms that opted out of the race or could not compete found themselves losing prestige and lawyers.

In the meantime, technology had become increasingly important to law firm management and legal research, and had changed the pace of legal practice and its expense. Paper court filings, and hand and mail deliveries, gave way to instantaneous faxes, then to electronic filings. Face-to-face meetings still occurred, but were supplemented by videoconferencing, e-mail, and other forms of electronic communication. Large firm libraries—formerly the physical and social hearts of the firms, and inhabited round the clock by industrious associates and even some partners—became empty chambers. By the 1990s computers rendered these quiet temples anachronistic and vestigial; maintaining them no longer made economic sense, either as a matter of hard-copy subscription costs or of square footage.

In short, the very physical structure of a lawyer's life, its daily texture, and its content, all transformed radically during the decades in which Frost grew up as a lawyer, took the reins of one of the nation's most powerful law firms, and held them for decades. Moreover, law practice has continued to transform at a dizzying pace since Frost left active practice in 1988. Gibson, Dunn & Crutcher has weathered these storms well, and today is one of the most powerful and respected law firms in the world. But to understand the law firm's evolution, as well as Frost's important contributions to its current success, requires a step back to the radically different world of the early 1950s.

✦ ✦ ✦

Frost's first days as a lawyer were spent in Pasadena, California, at the small firm of Boyle, Bissell and Atwill, which specialized in litigation and business law. In these early years Frost still was juggling the competing pulls between a life on the range and a life at the hub of economic and professional activity. Frost sought a middle road between them by beginning his career in a small town with a small practice. Drawing on his love of mathematics and aptitude for complex business transactions, he became a tax lawyer.

It took little time, however, for Frost to realize that his professional ambitions could not be fully realized in the slower-paced world of Pasadena. He had become an active member and officer of the Pasadena Bar Association, but he was restless and aware that Pasadena was not satisfying his needs.

In the fall of 1950, fate delivered the greatest opportunity of Frost's professional life. He was seated next to Homer Crotty, Gibson, Dunn & Crutcher senior partner and State Bar president, at a Pasadena Bar Association dinner, where he impressed the senior partner enough to prompt Crotty to arrange for the firm to interview Frost.

Frost appreciated the significance of such an opportunity, given Gibson, Dunn & Crutcher's reputation as a leading regional firm. The firm had a distinguished history by western standards, having been founded in 1890 by Judge John Bicknell and Walter Trask.[1] In 1897, Bicknell and Trask were joined by James Gibson; and in 1904, Bicknell, Gibson and Trask combined with William Dunn and Albert Crutcher to form what was then the largest law firm in Los Angeles. The Bicknell name was dropped after Bicknell's retirement in 1907, as was Trask's after his retirement in 1911, in conformance with the rules that then required that law firm names include only living, active partners. The name Gibson, Dunn & Crutcher endured.

The firm prospered over time and established deep roots in the California business community. And as Los Angeles grew, Gibson Dunn grew along with it. Indeed, the firm participated in nearly every aspect of Southern California's growth—from its earliest days as a small western outpost, to its rise to a sprawling metropolis and major economic hub. Consequently, an offer to join the firm was a major professional coup for any young California lawyer in the 1950s.

Here again, Frost's family ties provided a critical professional advantage: the senior Crotty had met Frost's parents and, before the life-altering Pasadena Bar Association dinner, was aware of their son's emerging legal career. Still another fortuity was that Frost was a tax lawyer. The law firm was specifically seeking to fortify its growing business practice. In short, Frost was in the right place, at the right time, with the right background and legal skills. He made the most of his chance, however, and Crotty invited Frost to Los Angeles to interview with other senior members of the firm.

The law firm's recruitment processes of that time were informal. There was no hiring committee, no summer associate program, no on-campus recruiting process. An interested lawyer typically would write to the firm requesting an interview, travel there at his own expense, and meet with a lawyer willing to take the time to interview the prospect. The firms typically hired from familiar sources: that is, graduates of law schools attended by partners of the firms, or the offspring of colleagues and acquaintances. Given these norms, Frost's family connections likely were essential to Crotty's initial willingness to interview him. University of Arizona graduates were less familiar to the members of this California-based firm than graduates of Ivy League or California law schools, where most of the partners had been trained.

During his interview, Frost met with several of the senior partners—most memorably with old-school, crusty Norman Sterry. By this time Frost already was married with an infant son and was worldly for his years, given his time overseas and his prior legal experience in Pasadena. Mr. Sterry, however, was unimpressed by these experiences. In fact, he squinted at Frost disapprovingly when he learned that Frost had a family. Sterry lectured Frost on how foolhardy it was to put anything ahead of one's professional duties and admonished him that the rigors and low pay of lawyering made marriage "irresponsible" for a young attorney.

The interview was a tough one that left Frost badly shaken. He feared Sterry would vote against hiring him because he was married and had a young son. But after Frost emerged from Sterry's office, he was reassured by the other senior lawyers that Sterry's surface gruffness belied a good heart. They explained, with some amusement, that Sterry's stern homily about a young lawyer's inability to manage both a career and a family was a standard trope that the older lawyer used on all young applicants. Sterry was more bark than bite, they chuckled, and a bit of a "character." They insisted that Frost need not worry.

The senior partners were right: Frost received an offer to join the firm, and he quickly accepted. He did so against the fatherly advice of lawyer Charlie Munger, who warned that the firm was "just too large" and that Frost would be "lost" there. Although a large firm by the standards of the day, the firm had only three dozen lawyers at the time and Munger's advice proved to be entirely off-base for Frost. From the start, Frost experienced the firm as highly collegial, and even when its size exceeded 500 lawyers in the late 1980s Frost regarded its members as a welcoming family—a place he later described as "stamped on my heart."

Despite his prior years of practice experience, Frost began his tenure at the firm on the bottom rung. He was the last name on the masthead, and earned only an entry-level associate's pay ($350/month). Like the other associates, he initially was given no office. Rather, he and the other associate "serfs" officed in the library, sharing desks, professional growing pains, and lively conversation about law and life. They brown-bagged lunches, carpooled to work, and supported each other through the boot camp phase of becoming a lawyer. Frost still remembers this era of his life with great fondness, primarily because of the camaraderie and collegiality of law practice in those days. The bonds forged among the young associates in the library were enduring ones.

Particularly vivid are his early memories of working for the formidable Norman Sterry. As Frost's first interview with Sterry had revealed, Sterry was an old-school lawyer in every respect. Sterry favored a rigorous Socratic method of mentoring young lawyers, which left an indelible impression on young Frost and his peers. Sterry trained protégés through probing questions rimmed with the threat of unmasking ignorance or, worse, a lack of conviction in one's research. Whenever Sterry issued an assignment, he conducted his own, independent research on the topic, plumbing footnotes and cross-references. He typically would lumber into the library on a late Friday afternoon and demand that one of the serfs prepare a legal memorandum "by Monday morning." Come Monday, the nervous associate would be summoned to Sterry's office and drilled thoroughly on all parts of his research. Sterry would try to bully the associate into changing his position and, as Frost recalls, "God help you if you changed your mind, or caved in." After this close interrogation, the exhausted associate finally would be excused and would return to the library to bind his wounds and seek consolation from his peers.

Despite the rigor and terror-inducing nature of Sterry's old-fashioned methods, the young associates knew that Sterry meant well. He took seriously his role as their mentor and teacher and believed the old methods were the best way to fortify them for the many rigors of law practice. Sterry was a product of his times, and Frost later credited Sterry's traditional methods with molding him into a lawyer who could conduct legal research at the highest level and hold his ground with the toughest superiors, judges, peers, and adversaries. He grew to regard Sterry as one of his most influential and effective teachers. Eventually, Frost became friends with his gruff taskmaster, and served as Sterry's personal lawyer in later years.

✦ ✦ ✦

In short order, Frost's combination of intellect, industry, and aptitude for business law made him a rising star within the firm. His analytical skills were well respected, and the senior lawyers trusted his research. The tax and probate department—not a strength of the firm when he arrived—became a powerful sector of the office that contributed to the firm's growing influence among corporate and industrial clients. Without it, the firm could not have offered these clients the sophisticated business-planning counsel they expected.

Frost also became what today is termed a "rainmaker" or "finder" within the firm. Law firm finders—usually midcareer to senior lawyers—develop business through professional networking, community activism, and strong reputations within the legal community. These finders typically need talented "minders"—junior partners and senior associates who "mind" the client's business in house—along with "grinders"—mid- to junior-level associates who do the daily "grind" work on the client's business. Frost—remarkably and quite distinctively—proved to be superb in all *three* roles very early in his career.

Once again, Frost leveraged his family connections to advance his professional goals and carried through in a way that generated good business. His father's connections to the leading brokerage houses and his mother's prominence among Pasadena social elites gave Frost an early opening for business development with many of their friends and associates. Of course, this entrée was only a first chance; Frost then had to prove himself. Yet these connections enabled Frost to bring clients with him from Pasadena even in his first days with the firm and to quickly develop new Los Angeles–based clients.

Context, too, worked in the neophyte lawyer's favor. At that time, the Southern California social and legal communities still were relatively intimate. This enabled Frost to make contacts easily and to rise quickly to leadership positions that displayed his talents to wider audiences.

Frost apprehended the importance of being proactive about

developing a reputation within one's field. In order to become better known, he added numerous writing and speaking engagements to his duties. He also produced many professional publications, including an article in the *Stanford Law Review*, that further established him as a leading thinker and practitioner in tax law and policy. These writings on tax law developments were much noticed, and drew new business to him and to the firm.

Frost also joined the Los Angeles County Bar Association's tax section, and soon became its chair. He became active at the state level, and again rose to a leadership post, as chair of the State Bar Tax Committee. At a young age, Frost already knew every prominent tax specialist in Los Angeles, and was known throughout the state of California. He delivered countless lectures on state and federal tax issues—to the California Franchise Tax Board, to the state Inheritance Tax Division, to related professional organizations, and to state and local CPA societies. He occasionally spoke to management consulting firms such as McKinsey, and was on the advisory committee to the Regional Commission of the Internal Revenue Service. (Later on, he was asked by President Nixon to become commissioner of the IRS, but he declined.) He became a respected figure among the major "Big Eight" accounting firms, and in other ways did the shoe-leather work of establishing himself as one of California's most experienced and insightful tax specialists. He was a member and eventual chair of the small Association of Tax Counsel of Los Angeles, made up of the most senior lawyers in the community. He was elected to the Board of the USC Tax Institute and spoke many times before the group. Finally, he was actively involved in various sections of the American Bar Association and contributed to the *ABA Journal*.

Indeed, by his late thirties, Frost had pursued nearly every bar-related post available to him and began to look outward to the Los Angeles community for other activities and endeavors. This all was exceedingly time-demanding, difficult work, especially for a young lawyer still learning his trade, but it had a tremendous professional yield. These external activities not only helped Frost to hone his legal skills; the exposure of the engagements also led to good business for Frost and for Gibson Dunn. Frost instinctively chose activities and attained influence in circles where major clients could be found, many of whom followed him back to the firm. In every venue, and in every situation, Frost seized the business development opportunity. He spoke, led, and excelled, and thereby increased his visibility and influence. This in turn broadened the firm's client base and influence.

✦   ✦   ✦

Taken together, Frost's legal skills, networking abilities, and exceptional work ethic set the stage for his ascendance to a leadership peg. He evidenced uncommon peripheral vision about opportunities, and was able to turn his many social and professional connections into business opportunities. Frost also had the energy and capacity to follow through for his colleagues and clients and place them at the center of his attention in an unblinking way. Finally, Frost had good mentors and good fortune.

His early years as a lawyer highlight the degree to which his professional success required personal self-sacrifice. Frost made his work a primary, sometimes exclusive, priority in order to reach the highest rungs as a lawyer at Gibson Dunn. In this respect, Norm Sterry was absolutely correct: a decision to pursue this life inevitably affected a young lawyer's ability to minister to family and others. Frost understood this from the start, and applied himself eagerly and fully to the task. He was an uncommonly determined man whose will to succeed was exceptional, even indomitable.

✦ ✦ ✦

California as Context

Frost's professional success also was aided by his California and Los Angeles setting. Pasadena offered Frost a decent life as a lawyer, but it could not begin to match Los Angeles in terms of its growth trajectory. Because Frost knew this limitation, he appreciated the significance of his meeting with Homer Crotty in 1950 and the chance to move to a new setting with better opportunities.

Frost had seen the importance of context from his own childhood experiences and that of his relatives. He recalled how his Blackburn great-grandfather and uncles had sacrificed economic opportunities by remaining rooted in the rural Paso Robles area. Although he admired and respected his Blackburn relatives, he understood that one must be willing to move into the vortex of a more vibrant and rapidly growing urban center in order to achieve one's most ambitious professional goals.

In 1950, the population of the greater Los Angeles–Riverside–Orange County area was almost 5 million. This was still an outpost in many respects—it was nine years away from the arrival of the jet airplane and the rise of more rapid transcontinental air travel. But it was a growing metropolis in Southern California, and in only forty-five years the population rose a whopping 221.5 percent, to almost 15.5 million. In the same period, the population of the New York metropolitan area rose only 42 percent, and the Chicago area rose only 25 percent. The West, Southwest, and South all vastly outstripped the East and Midwest in growth during the decades of Frost's career. The Los Angeles area thus offered an uncommonly rich base for legal entrepreneurs, as well as people seeking business opportunities.

California's post–World War II growth stemmed in significant part from military production, the growth of air travel, and the surge in technology and need for skilled labor. Major aerospace leaders such as Douglas, Lockheed, and North American built their primary operations in California. The G.I. Bill, and the beginnings of the "knowledge based economy," placed greater emphasis on an educated workforce. The latter fueled the need for, and widespread support of, California's exceptional public and private colleges and universities. Agriculture, long a dominant sector of California's economy, also continued to be a backbone of the state's growth and prosperity, and was itself a locus of significant academic research. The long coastline provided fishing, real estate, and tourism advantages, and added to the state's image as a place for escape to the beauty and adventure of the great Pacific. And, of course, the entertainment industry is most closely identified with Hollywood. The motion picture industry's studio system of the pre-1950s gave way to new structures of film distribution and actor engagement, and California overcame New York's early lead as the center of the new television industry, capturing the lion's share of the television medium.

All of these developments contributed to California's rapid ascendance as a major economic power. By the start of the twenty-first century, California was the ninth largest economy *in the world*.

However California's financial fortunes went, so went the nation's—if not the globe's. The West Coast had clearly arrived.

If Frost's Andover days tutored him in the East Coast's intellectual and social dominance, subsequent decades opened his eyes to a new, bicoastal imperialism in the United States. California became the undisputed anchor of emerging West Coast influence, and Los Angeles overtook San Francisco as the most muscular California city during this surge in western economic power. Los Angeles and California therefore were not just good places for Frost to build his professional career during this period in American history; they arguably were the best possible places to build a career in these years. The thriving economy, emerging industries, excellent public and private schools, and spectacularly beautiful vistas made this California location nearly irresistible to business investors and inventors.

California also was a cauldron of creativity and innovation. As the social revolutions of the 1960s and 1970s hit, California became the locus of cultural foment, adding to its allure as a place that invited change, even unrest. For younger Americans—whose inventiveness and energy fuel the nation's economic and cultural future, and whose life chances have determined the quality of the nation's workforce, productivity, and leadership pool—California was nearly unique in the range of opportunities it offered for a successful, prosperous, and meaningful professional life.

Indeed, California in the postwar era emerged as its own, very modern, culture. It became a distinctive medley of the cultures of its nineteenth-century past, along with an embrace of the new, the outré, and the entrepreneurial. The state faced outward literally and figuratively, which nurtured its identity and sense of itself as other, open-ended, "golden."

For a lawyer, the business and professional opportunities in California during this time seemed nearly endless. The rise of larger corporations and of new industries led to an urgent need for savvy business counsel to assist business actors in framing new corporate and intellectual property structures, nurturing their start-ups, guiding their mergers and acquisitions, managing their sophisticated corporate and securities transactions, and representing them in their large-scale corporate litigation and class actions. Booming real estate and other expanding businesses in California likewise needed talented lawyers at the table. The vigorous California economy provided great spectacular grist for lawyers' mills.

Gibson, Dunn & Crutcher rode this California wave ably. It chose its niche and carved its path as a firm willing to grow with the times. Its leaders, especially Frost, understood that where traditional law firms were loath to travel, other lawyers would rush in. These new times meant new business, but also new competition. Gibson Dunn was not about to cede this turf, however, and Frost in particular dedicated himself to establishing the California law firm as one of the nation's most powerful.

Rather than overcoming the firm's western location, the law firm began to leverage it. The iconic image of a more "laid back" California culture actually served the firm's ambitious new goals. It touted this culture as part of the Gibson, Dunn & Crutcher difference from East Coast (read: New York City) competitors. A less staid atmosphere was embraced as the firm grew in self-confidence and national stature.

The firm's members also cited the economic vibrancy of their West Coast clients when recruiting new lawyers. These emerging West Coast industries, they emphasized, offered lucrative business, interesting clients, and intellectually engaging, pathbreaking legal work. California promised cutting-edge legal issues for lawyers representing Napa's emerging wine industry, Silicon Valley's technology gurus, the rapidly evolving film and television industry, and other distinctively California-based concerns.

The tenor of the times more generally fortified the younger coast's competitive edge and growing swagger. As the nation embraced more democratic and innovation-embracing ideals, this made California seem more attractive to young professionals. Even traditionally change-averse legal professionals began to reject socioeconomic, cultural, and religious status as the primary determinants of success and access, in favor of more meritocratic and openly competitive measures. Elite law schools underwent demographic and cultural transformations that resulted in fewer graduates who believed that the best practice destinations were solely the handful of elite, expensive, white-shoe, and mostly WASP law firms in New York or Boston. "Sweat equity" and merit began to supplant "social equity" and connections, which opened the doors of even top firms to accomplished graduates from more modest family backgrounds.

The expanding function of in-house counsel within major corporations also played a role in displacing older models of the law firm pecking order. In-house lawyers cared, above all, about the price and quality of the legal work that external counsel could provide, and few cared much about these lawyers' social pedigrees. Large law firms began to compete for corporate business, as these in-house lawyers became far more sophisticated and demanding consumers of outside counsel expertise. Social connections still mattered to the law firms, especially elite ones; but "connections" began to be redefined in ways beyond social class. Connections that mattered to business development could include connections to minority business owners, to law school classmates who had opted for in-house work and thus had a say in choosing outside counsel, to government officials, and to a range of others who might generate referrals.

It would be a mistake, however, to assume that established California firms were free from old school biases or embraced this new social order overnight. Many were populated with eastern school graduates, such that the habits of the eastern firms had western tentacles as well. If anything, the more a western law firm craved respectability, the more it tended to imitate the instincts and elitism of the distinguished firms of the East. The older California firms in particular often mimicked the norms, attitudes, and prejudices of the established East Coast firms, including their emphasis on Ivy League pedigrees and family connections.

Consequently, Gibson Dunn suffered growing pains when the traditional social order and mores of the legal profession began to crater. Some of its senior partners, though surely not all of them, shared the insular recruitment, promotion, and firm management attitudes of the pre-1950s. In the early 1950s, one of the firm's senior partners offered Sandra Day O'Connor—Stanford law superstar and future U.S. Supreme Court justice—a position as a legal secretary instead of as a lawyer. The anecdote is retold in nearly every account of O'Connor's historic career. Finding no position in any California private firm—at Gibson Dunn or elsewhere—O'Connor accepted a job as deputy county attorney for San Mateo, California. Years later, however, it was Gibson Dunn senior partner William French Smith who offered crucial support to her nomination to the Court, when he served as U.S. attorney general.

Concerns about lingering exclusionary attitudes once led Stanford Law School to ban Gibson Dunn from conducting on-campus interviews there. The ground was an alleged anti-Semitic remark by a senior partner. Again, the incident did not reflect the views of the firm as a whole, or of fellow partners at the time (including Frost). It nevertheless fueled the impression that the firm was resistant to changing attitudes and caused significant internal consternation. The firm thereafter took steps to expand lawyer diversity and to prevent bias. It made high-profile lateral hires, as well as entry-level hires, that altered the firm's demographics and restored its reputation as forward thinking and acting. One striking example of this occurred in the 1970s, when Frost approached Paul Ziffren, a well-known and politically connected Jewish lawyer in California, and persuaded him to join the firm. Although Ziffren's hire initially made waves, his exceptional performance quieted naysayers. Ziffren later became chairman of the U.S. Olympic Committee, among other accomplishments, and his ties to Hollywood and Democratic Party elites provided business development opportunities for Gibson Dunn. Women began to be actively recruited, mentored, and promoted to partner, and lawyers of color began to join the firm's ranks as well.

By the 1980s, Gibson Dunn embraced diversity as one of its central goals and values. The firm expanded the pool of lawyers, changed the face of its members, and preserved its status and influence. Like other national law firms in the latter decades of the twentieth century,[1] leading California firms steadily shed antimeritocratic practices in order to stay competitive and contemporary, to respond to social changes, and to respect evolving standards of the profession. To be sure, some of the changes were at first more rhetorical than actual—the ranks of many firms at all levels remained predominantly white, and at the level of partnership the number of women also lagged. Yet a noteworthy transformation in lawyer attitudes and law firm hiring practices did occur in the 1970s and 1980s, even in old-line California firms. Gibson Dunn reflected these evolving professional patterns.

Still another transformation during the postwar era was that the iconic lawyer no longer was a solo litigator in an "Atticus Finch," a Clarence Darrow, or even a "Perry Mason" vein. Rather, the business lawyer and large case litigator—think *L.A. Law*—became new paradigms. Law as a profession—as a calling—no longer was seen as inconsistent with law as a business. Leaders in the profession began to openly embrace law firms as for-profit endeavors that required managers to quantify, reward, and advance aggressively the firm's profitability. The very definition of "professionalism" underwent momentous reform, as leaders of firms everywhere began to push this envelope by unselfconsciously emphasizing billing, client development, marketing, and outreach in order to protect the firm's financial well-being and attract major business clients.

Finally, the postwar era brought a sea change in terms of the physical locations of leading American firms. Major firms discovered that they needed to establish offices across the country in order to attract, retain, and serve their clients. For Los Angeles firms, this not only meant that they needed to look east for possible expansion, but that New York and other eastern-based firms began to look west for new outposts. In the early 1980s, New York firms began to open offices in California rather than refer west-based clients to California firms. To staff the new offices, they engaged in aggressive recruiting of California lawyers and pursued a wider network of clients to support these new branches. Some firms were destroyed in the battle for talent and business, including the 100-lawyer firm of Kadison, Pfaelzer, Woodard, Quinn & Rossi, which disappeared in 1987. The survivors—which included Gibson, Dunn & Crutcher—were the firms that adapted rapidly to the new pressures.

Frost is widely credited as the primary person at Gibson Dunn who forged the firm's counteroffensive and growth strategy during this period of external challenges. Drawing on his experience with the firm's earlier expansion efforts—Herb Sturdy had tasked Frost with leading the firm's entry into the overseas market when Frost was a young lawyer—he pushed outward in multiple directions. According to Ken Doran, the firm's current managing partner, Frost was a key actor in the firm's establishment of a D.C. office in 1977. Frost later also superintended the firm's moves into multiple other markets across the United States and overseas.

Ronald Beard—who later became a managing partner—recalls approaching Frost after Beard returned from a trip to London in the spring of 1979. Beard was convinced that the firm should establish a presence there and went to Frost to make the case for such a move.

Plans were already in the works, however, and the firm opened its doors to the London office less than one year later. Frost was one of the few senior partners, says Beard, who saw clearly the need for the firm's expansion into this and other markets from the start.

This expansion of the firm to multiple new venues enabled it to better weather the ensuing financial storms, which then typically had more local, industry-specific impacts than nationally or globally pervasive ones. For example, when natural resource business was booming, the firm's Denver office reflected that spurt, and offset losses in other parts of the economy that were felt more deeply elsewhere in the nation. The Denver office also enabled the firm to better serve its telephone and communications clients. The firm's Dallas office likewise was strategic: it was created to benefit from the growing financial power of Texas, and to fortify the firm's ability to represent another signature client—American Airlines. In sum, Frost understood "hedging" as a financial strategy and deployed it with finesse when selecting new office venues. His growth strategy produced a healthier overall bottom line for the firm. Above all, his decision to open a New York City office in the early 1980s enabled the firm to defend itself from the East Coast invasion.[2]

✦ ✦ ✦

If the pace of early twentieth-century legal practice quickened to a trot after World War II, it broke into a full gallop by the close of the twentieth century. Lawyers and law firm leaders who did not anticipate and adapt to this change in pace were doomed to minor influence or, worse, to failure and dissolution of the firm. The globalization of business led to a "flattening" of the world itself, and globalism became a nonabstract imperative of law firm practice and planning. "Location" still mattered enormously to one's economic opportunity by the 1980s, but it began to be less actual than virtual, less physical than attitudinal, less regional than global. Here, too,

Gibson Dunn anticipated the shifts. Frost in particular anticipated all of it; indeed, he seemed destined to anticipate it, given his life experiences and exceptional ability to adapt to changes in his external environment.

The peripatetic grooming of young Frost—moving from school to school, coast to coast, domestic to foreign soil, dew-soaked to desert environments, private to public schools, frontier to elite social settings, rural to refined worlds—gave him an unusual and highly useful ability to move with the shifts of the 1950s through the 1980s, to quickly adjust to new locations and to a range of new cultures, business needs, and contexts. Frost was rarely distracted by what, on the surface, seemed stable and crucial. He could identify quickly and accurately what in fact was working (or *not* working) in a given situation and predict where the new winds were blowing. Despite the force of change, he adhered consistently to a specific goal: professional success, defined by good outcomes for his client and profitability for his lawyers. Most notably, Frost did not define success locally or even regionally; he leveraged location to reach beyond its confines. He was uncommonly cosmopolitan and worldly in his tasks, as evidenced by his early embrace of Eastern cultures during his time overseas.

California in the postwar era thus was a perfect location for Frost *in particular*. It was defined both by where it was—in a hub of growth and innovation, of booms and busts—and where it was not—fixed in the tradition-based, historically rich, eastern American corridor. It faced out, to a seemingly limitless global horizon—to the ocean and to the Pacific Basin, rather than to Western Europe. It also faced into the ether, to a virtual world increasingly connected by technology and airwaves, rather than by visible, traditional cords. At the same time, it was and still remains spectacularly vulnerable to the forces of Nature. The state is perched tentatively on underlying fault lines and buffeted regularly by cycles of drought, fires, and mudslides. It likewise is vulnerable to economic peaks and deep valleys, and subject to the social and political internal pressures of its sprawling and diverse population. Although its enduring image is that of a frontier, with open spaces and the chance to see light and life anew, only those tough enough to tame that mercurial place and who can see beyond its many illusions actually succeed there.

Frost understood all of this. He clearly saw California's great potential, but he also appreciated its perils, its problems, and its fragility. He witnessed the rise of the California industrial complex, the stirring demographic and cultural transformations, the spike in population, and the succession of staggering domestic and global conflicts. He saw the legal profession undergo dramatic change. He understood that all of these powerful forces had to be heeded for his firm to succeed. This was the context in which Frost lived and worked, and from which he later propelled Gibson Dunn outward, to the world.

CHAPTER FIVE

✦ ✦ ✦

Client-Centered

Every major law firm is defined by its stable of clients—by their profitability, their industries, their reputations, their fortunes, their losses. Every lawyer, too, is shaped by his or her personal clients. For a business lawyer in the twentieth century, individual clients' personalities often mattered enormously to the engagement, because many major businesses still were dominated by single individuals rather than by remote, faceless boards. Many lawyers became trusted personal advisors to their prominent clients and in some cases became close friends who participated in their clients' lives, attended family events, enjoyed mutual interests beyond work, and shared the passage from middle-age vitality and adventures to end-of-life estate planning and matters of business succession.

Frost was this kind of hands-on business lawyer par excellence. His expertise as a business and tax specialist afforded him especially close relationships with many prominent clients, because his duties often involved him in the complex intersection between his clients' business and personal affairs. Frost consistently exercised the skill, prudence, and good judgment that one needs in a lawyer, and hopes for in a family friend. Above all, he earned their trust, which often led them to ask him to handle other important business matters for their family and business.

Frost especially enjoyed the clients who were entrepreneurs during their active years. He experienced them as among the most dynamic and creative individuals he encountered as a lawyer, as the ones whose intellects he most admired, and as the ones whose energy and aptitude for cultivating significant wealth he found most captivating. Indeed, Frost himself later went from advising such clients to trying his own hand at several business concerns, in order to satisfy his personal urge to build entities in addition to the law firm he helped to fortify, then expand.

What follows are Frost's recollections of his most intriguing and significant client engagements. The snapshots are of the clients who, by Frost's lights, most affected his development as a lawyer and as a person. His narratives reveal that Frost often began a client relationship by offering tax and business advice to an individual, which eventually led to the firm's engagement on a host of other legal matters for the client and his corporate concerns. In several notable instances, Frost represented the client for decades and became not only a trusted lawyer to the client and his family, but a board member for the client's businesses or charitable foundations.

The following snapshots also illustrate the profound commitment to others' interests that a lawyer's life can entail. Frost's client relationships not only required him to manage the client's business needs ably; he also had to fathom and attend to the client's personal needs as well. This took psychological insight, interpersonal skills, and time. The countless hours Frost spent managing his clients' business concerns—as well as understanding their personalities, interests, antipathies, and passions—were a worthwhile professional investment, to be sure. But this time could not be given away twice. It is little surprise that Frost's clients became an extension of Frost himself, and helped to shape his own identity.

The Paul Hoffman Family

The Paul G. Hoffman family and related business and charitable concerns initially came to Frost through family ties. His primary link was to Lathrop Hoffman, whom Frost had met in Pasadena.

Lathrop's father, Paul, was for many years the president and CEO of the Studebaker Corporation, which was headquartered in South Bend, Indiana. The Hoffman family also owned the Studebaker distributorship in Los Angeles, which later was managed by Lathrop.[1]

Paul Hoffman was active in governmental circles and became a personal friend of presidents Roosevelt and Truman. At the end of World War II, President Truman created the Marshall Plan to provide food, technical help, and funds to restore the economic health of Europe. He placed the former chief of staff of U.S. Forces in World War II, General George Marshall, in charge of the operation. President Truman and General Marshall asked Hoffman to take a leave of absence from the Studebaker Corporation and become the administrator of the Marshall Plan in Europe. Hoffman agreed and, as is well known, the plan was an enormous success. During this time, Hoffman also became a great friend and admirer of General Dwight D. Eisenhower, who was then head of NATO.

In 1951, Hoffman joined a movement consisting of many distinguished citizens, both within the government and in the private sector, to persuade Eisenhower to run for president against Harry Truman. The movement was successful, and Eisenhower resigned as head of NATO and returned to the United States to assess the feasibility of a presidential campaign.

This Eisenhower for President movement affected Frost personally. One day in 1951 Frost was summoned to the office of Elmo Conley, an important senior partner and head of the firm's

Tax/Probate Department. When Frost entered Conley's office, he found it filled with several distinguished men and one very attractive woman, who was introduced to him as Jackie Cochran. The men included Paul Hoffman; Paul Helms, owner of the then largest bakery in Southern California; Tom Knudsen, owner of the then largest milk and cheese company in Southern California; and Floyd Odlum, who was married to Jackie Cochran. Sitting quietly in the corner was General Dwight D. Eisenhower and members of his staff.

The purpose of the meeting was to discuss the creation of a collateral organization to the Republican Party to be called "Citizens for Ike." Cochran was to be in charge of the California unit of "Citizens for Ike," and the group had decided that Cochran needed legal advice with regard to the election laws and similar matters. Frost was assigned to the post of legal advisor and traveling companion for Cochran as she traveled around California.

To put it mildly, Frost notes wryly, this was a difficult assignment. Cochran was an outspoken, independent, and fiery woman who was rightfully proud of her many accomplishments. She was then the most famous aviatrix in the world, the head of the Women's Army Corps, and holder of several world speed records in both propeller and jet fighters. She also was a great friend of the famous air force generals of World War II and, through these friendships, once "borrowed" the latest jet fighter in order to set a world speed record for a woman aviator.

Frost performed his legal duties as assigned, and accompanied Cochran across California. He remembers nightly calls from Floyd Odlum to see how his "girl" was doing, and how Cochran stirred controversy within the existing Republican hierarchy in California, some of whom resented having no control over her actions. She was extremely effective, however, in creating groups independent of the Republican Party under the banner "Citizens for Ike," and subsequently was transferred to the national office of the organization. Frost then returned to his normal lawyering duties at the firm, but remained an active campaigner for Eisenhower thereafter and never forgot his campaign experience.[2]

Frost's legal relationship with the Paul Hoffman businesses began early in Frost's career, when Hoffman's son Lathrop and his wife, Dorothy, began their estate planning and asked Frost to become their legal counsel. This legal relationship then was transferred to Gibson Dunn when Frost joined the firm,[3] and Frost subsequently carried out a number of other legal assignments for the Hoffman Company and for Paul Hoffman individually. Frost also joined the Paul G. Hoffman Company Board, where he served for many years.

Of all the duties Frost performed for the Hoffmans, he is most proud of his work for the Ford Foundation, at which Paul Hoffman served as the first president. The Ford Foundation set up several sub-foundations, including the famous Fund for Adult Education. This fund stimulated the creation of public television stations throughout the country and was headed by the late Bill Griffiths, who also became a close friend of Frost. The two traveled together extensively in carrying out the mandate of the fund, which was to provide initial financing for public stations to be matched by local contributions. Frost created the contractual arrangements for the public stations and supervised the fulfillment of the conditions necessary to receive a grant. Through this assignment, Frost came to know the founders of virtually all of the major public television stations in the United States, especially those in principal cities and university communities.

The Times Mirror Company

As the years went by, Frost met many more high-profile clients and dignitaries. He grew in experience and stature within the firm, and quickly graduated from "the library." He even began delegating some of his work to other lawyers and, in 1956, he was promoted to first-tier partner after only five years with the firm.

What catapulted Frost over other, more senior colleagues were his ability to attract good business, his extensive community outreach, and his dedication to his clients. Frost had a natural instinct for business development and, as mentioned earlier, was willing to devote the countless hours of nonbillable time to networking and building contacts. He belonged to multiple social organizations, wrote numerous professional articles, and gave substantive speeches in venues where business clients would hear him address issues of concern to them and might later consult with him on these legal issues. One of these early speaking occasions led to one of the firm's and Frost's most important and influential clients—the Los Angeles Times Mirror Company.

Frost delivered a lecture about qualified stock options at a seminar put on by McKinsey & Company. These options then were a relatively new vehicle for executive compensation, and the seminar was aimed at chief financial officers. Among the guests at the seminar was Omar Johnson—then the chief financial officer and treasurer of Times Mirror. Johnson was so impressed by Frost's remarks that he later arranged for the young Gibson, Dunn & Crutcher partner to meet with the senior management of Times Mirror to discuss handling of the company's qualified executive stock option plans and executive incentive plans. Frost's meeting with the management group was a complete success, and Gibson Dunn was hired to prepare a stock option plan for Times Mirror.

The company stock then was listed over the counter, with a very small trading volume. However, changes were stirring at the company. Under McKinsey's suggestion, as consultants to Times Mirror, three new outside directors were added to the company board, all prominent members of the Los Angeles and national business community—Tex Thornton, CEO of Litton Industries; Frank King, CEO of California Bank; and Harry Volk, CEO of Union Bank.

When Frost was asked to explain the new executive compensation plan to the Times Mirror Board, he made his presentation to the three new directors, along with the rest of the board. This was a daunting task for a young lawyer; Tex Thornton at that time was considered one of the most brilliant, sophisticated, and aggressive CEOs in the country.[4]

Frost impressed the board and got the assignment. He enlisted Frank Wheat, a close friend and corporate securities partner, who later became an SEC commissioner, to prepare the documents, and their work on this initial assignment led to other work for the company, as well as an invitation to Frost to become general counsel to Times Mirror. Frost declined the offer and recommended instead a young associate at the firm, Robert F. Erburu, who accepted the job and later became CEO of Times Mirror.

Gibson Dunn became general outside counsel for Times Mirror, and this representation continued until the sale of the company to the *Chicago Tribune* several decades later. Frost also was asked to represent the Chandler Trusts, Chandis Securities Company, Norman and Dorothy B. Chandler, and other various senior members of the Chandler family, including the surviving six children of Harry Chandler,[5] and he also joined the Times Mirror Board.

Frost believes the Chandler family—known for their powerful personalities and diverse political opinions—was held together by their respect for their older brother, Norman Chandler. Norman served as chairman of the trustees and of Chandis Securities Company and was very important to the success of the newspaper and to the diversification efforts of the Times Mirror Company. Frost describes Chandler as a man with a wide circle of friends and business acquaintances, who was well respected by the employees of the Times Mirror. Frost also believes that Chandler's contributions to the success of the company were greatly underrated. For example, Chandler selected as his executive editor the famous Nick

Williams—whom Frost regards as one of the greatest executive editors in the history of the *Los Angeles Times*.

In 1960, Norman Chandler named his son, Otis, to succeed him as publisher of the *Los Angeles Times*. Norman then became president of the Times Mirror Company and was extremely active in the company's efforts to reduce the company's dependence on the newspaper business alone and to diversify its newspaper business geographically by acquiring newspapers around the country. During this time the Times Mirror Company also expanded into book publishing, television, flight maps, the general map business, law book publishing, and many other businesses. In due course, the company was listed on the New York Stock Exchange with Series A and Series B stock capitalization.

Frost's last meeting with Norman Chandler, which occurred shortly before Chandler's death, was a particularly poignant moment. Chandler had developed cancer and in late 1973 underwent major surgery. The afternoon before the surgery, he asked Frost to join him and his wife at their home in order to review his estate plan. After the meeting, Chandler walked Frost to his car—which never had happened before—and was in a very serious mood. Frost believes Chandler had a premonition that he would not survive the surgery, which turned out to be correct. He bid Frost an affectionate good night and then drew from his pocket a small package. The package contained a pair of gold cuff links that Chandler had worn for many years. Frost was deeply moved and has worn the cuff links ever since.

Norman Chandler's son, Otis, served as publisher from 1960 to 1980. According to Frost, Otis resigned as publisher due to health reasons, after which he served as chairman of Times Mirror until his retirement in 1986. Otis was succeeded as publisher by Tom Johnson.[6]

From 1960 to 1980, under Otis Chandler as publisher and

Nick Williams as executive editor, the *Los Angeles Times* continued to prosper and substantially increased its circulation and advertising revenues. This success continued under Tom Johnson as publisher, and later under David Laventhol, who was publisher when Frost retired from the board in 1992 at the mandatory retirement age of seventy.[7]

Gibson Dunn handled a wide range of important business for Times Mirror while Frost was at the firm. For example, when Times Mirror went on its acquisition spree, this generated new mergers and acquisitions business for Gibson Dunn lawyers. The paper acquired franchises in Baltimore, Dallas, and Hartford, all of which were under water. This work in turn led to the firm's representation of the paper in important First Amendment cases. In time, the firm also handled the paper's labor relations in its notorious struggles with union organizers, as well as other employment issues. In short, what began as Frost's tax advice matter for Times Mirror ultimately blossomed into full-service representation of the diverse legal affairs of a major Gibson Dunn client.

Frost's relationship with the Chandlers also blossomed, and he served on the Times Mirror Board for a quarter century. In this role, Frost worked to advance the paper's prestige and its future profitability as the paper dealt with the pressures of a changing industry. He became both a witness to the internal debates of a major newspaper during this period, and a participant in key decision-making.[8]

Through service on the Times Mirror Board, Frost met many other important businesspeople—some of whom later became clients of the firm. Most notably, the Times Mirror top officers included Al Casey, executive vice-president, and Dennis Stanfill, chief financial officer, who later became chief executive officers of American Airlines and Fox Studios, respectively.[9]

Frost also met the daughter of Norman Chandler—Camilla ("Mia") Chandler—during his time on the board, and the two eventually became good friends. After Frost and his wife divorced, and Mia separated from her husband, the two began a courtship that resulted in their marriage in 1975.

This high-profile, well-connected couple appeared often in the Los Angeles elite business, social, and arts scenes. Mia Chandler was active on the boards of Cal-Tech, a trustee of Wellesley College, and the head of the Los Angeles County Museum of Art. Frost also became very active in the local community and became a board member and officer of the Los Angeles Music Center, and as president of the Music Center Foundation. The latter group was a veritable "who's who" of the Southern California business elite, and was created by Frost and Dr. Peter Bing at the behest of Dorothy ("Buff") Chandler. Under their leadership, the foundation grew to more than $100 million in assets. Frost also served on the Walt Disney Concert Hall Committee, was a member of the Los Angeles 100 Club, and the Committee of 25—all on top of his professional responsibilities. The planning of Disney Hall was an especially lengthy and complex matter in which Frost played a key, early role. Frost, along with Lew Wasserman, caused the county property on which the hall is located to be saved from commercial development, after an intense fight. Frost also was instrumental in securing the Disney leadership gift for the project. Reflecting on these contributions, Dr. Bing has described Frost as "the person who made Disney Hall possible" and has stated that "because it was [Frost] who spearheaded this project, a lot of others got behind it as well." Frost's leadership on the project was "manna from heaven," and the finished hall helped Los Angeles "to lure the new conductor [Dudamel], who, in turn, is luring great crowds as Zubin Mehta did in his day." Frost's early work on Disney Hall helped to transform the arts culture of Los Angeles, as well as the city's architecture.

In sum, the Times Mirror connection was profoundly life altering for Frost. He met important new clients, developed deep and abiding friendships, met and married Mia Chandler, and became an important player on the Los Angeles cultural scene. He also was a participant in the growth of a nationally respected media company during its most influential years and was a close confidant and advisor to one of Southern California's most powerful families of all time—the Chandlers.

Don Haskell, Tejon Ranch

Frost's demanding life of a downtown Los Angeles lawyer and community leader afforded him precious little time for other pursuits. Although he still loved the out of doors and made what time he could for recreation, his opportunities to escape from work were infrequent.

His client and friend Donald Haskell thus was a tonic for him. Haskell was a great himself, and was instrumental in providing Frost with some of the most memorable out-of-office experiences of Frost's life, as well as interesting legal business.

Haskell was the nephew of Arnold Haskell, through whom Don had become chairman of California's sprawling Tejon Ranch. The story of Uncle Arnold's rise to affluence was a classic Horatio Alger tale—one that deserves its own, separate book. A short version of this full life is that Arnold worked for M. H. Sherman, a well-known Los Angeles financier who made a fabulous fortune in real estate and other ventures in Southern California during the early 1900s.

Known as "General Sherman," M. H. Sherman had been the adjutant general in the territory of Arizona before it became a state in early 1912. Sherman started a streetcar business in Phoenix, but concluded that the dusty and still minor Arizona city was too small a venue for his loftiest aspirations. He moved to Los Angeles, where he quickly bought up significant amounts of land in partnership with Norman Chandler's father, Harry Chandler of the *Los Angeles Times*. One of their joint business ventures was Tejon Ranch—more than 200,000 acres of ranch land located one hour north of Los Angeles.[10]

Arnold was an accountant by training, and a wily fellow. As the story goes, he began as General Sherman's driver. Arnold bribed Sherman's houseman in Hancock Park to advise Arnold whenever Sherman was about to leave the premises. Once alerted that Sherman was preparing to exit the house, Arnold would pull Sherman's car out of the garage and start polishing it. Every time the general emerged from his home, he found Arnold polishing his car. Arnold's industriousness so impressed Sherman that he eventually promoted Arnold to become his chief assistant.

Arnold's assistant duties for General Sherman included management of Arnold's business affairs, and the care of Sherman's three daughters, none of whom had married and all of whom lived in Spain. When the general died, he left a very substantial trust for the daughters and other interests, and named Arnold Haskell as trustee.

Haskell thereafter continued to manage the interests of the three Sherman daughters and the estate, as promised. When he approached the end of his own life, he looked for a successor to manage the Sherman business interests and turned to his nephew, Don. Arnold asked his nephew to assume responsibility for managing the Sherman trusts, overseeing the Sherman Gardens, and overseeing the library in Laguna Beach.

Don then was a practicing dentist and was not completely sold on the idea of forgoing his profession. He decided to strike a bargain with his uncle—one that would later benefit Frost as well. The bargain was that Don would agree to take over the management of Arnold's business affairs if Arnold would do two things. First, he would buy the *Chubasco*, a magnificent wooden sloop that had won the Trans-Pac Race and was built and owned by the Stewart family, founders of Union Oil Company. Second, he would fund a yacht brokerage in Newport Beach. The uncle agreed to Don's terms, bought the historic vessel *Chubasco*, and funded the yacht brokerage—later called "Ardell" Marine, a play on the name Arnold Haskell.

Ardell Marine eventually became the largest yacht brokerage in the world and Don Haskell extensively raced the *Chubasco* on both coasts and in the Mediterranean and cruised many parts of the world. On several of these high seas adventures, he was joined by his lawyer and friend, Dan Frost.

Frost's business relationship with Haskell began in the early 1960s, when Frost represented Tejon Ranch in various tax matters.[11] Gibson Dunn later represented Tejon Ranch as general counsel.

Tejon Ranch historically derived its revenue from oil and gas, its cattle operations, the sale of hunting rights, an extensive farming and orchard operation after the advent of the California Water Project, and the commercial development of real estate along both sides of Interstate 5. The ranch became a public company listed on the American Stock Exchange, though there never was a public offering of its shares. Rather, as the founders died, their families sold off shares of stock and, gradually, there came to be several thousand stockholders. The largest single holding was held by the descendants of General Sherman through various trusts and individual holdings. Don Haskell was the representative of the Sherman holdings on the Board of Tejon, and its chairman.

Frost and the law firm represented Tejon Ranch in matters involving water rights, oil and gas, and ranching affairs; the gradual development of its land holdings; protection of boundaries to the extent possible from the encroachment of federal, state, and private claims; and the negotiation of large easements with all of the major California utility companies that wanted to traverse ranch property to deliver their products to the Los Angeles market. Once again, a Frost connection to an important businessman began with tax advice, then led to significant new business for the firm.

R. Stanton Avery

Client Don Haskell offered Frost the gift of high seas adventure, and the Chandler family offered him the gift of exceptional community, cultural, and personal connections. Client R. Stanton Avery offered Frost fundamental life lessons about entrepreneurial leadership and legacies. Indeed, Avery became Frost's most important professional role model and teacher.

The first Avery lesson was that a successful entrepreneur anticipates future business needs and invents new ways of responding to these as-yet nascent needs. In some cases, Frost observed, an entrepreneur actually can create a need that his or her invention or investment will address.

The second Avery lesson was that all people have a duty to give back to the world, and that successful people should seek to "do good wholesale, not by retail." Avery had a spectacularly generous soul, and concluded early in his life that he might best effect positive social change by leveraging his phenomenal inventive talents to first create significant wealth, then direct it to important philanthropies. This became Avery's greatest and most enduring legacy.

Avery's own muses in terms of his philanthropic philosophy included his first wife, the daughter of a minister, and his father, who also was a minister. Dorothy Durfee Avery believed the biblical adage that it is "easier for a camel to go through the eye of a needle than for a rich man to go to heaven." For this reason, she had profound ambivalence about her husband's march to great wealth, and reinforced in him the obligation to share his good fortune with others.

Avery's inventive genius derived, he believed, from his "Yankee inventor" ancestors. His grandfather was an expert clockmaker who built magnificent timepieces and patented the "Avery clock." Avery wedded this inventive heritage with his religious training throughout his adult life. After his graduation from Pomona College, he went to work for the Los Angeles County Welfare Department. There, he confronted daily the ravages of poverty and did what he could—albeit one by one—to assist. But he soon realized he could accomplish far more in his life, and promote greater social welfare, if he first used his natural genius to create a profitable business. Avery borrowed $100.00 from his future wife, rented space over a flower shop in a low rent district in Los Angeles, and began developing the world's first pressure-sensitive, quick-release paper. There, Avery designed the first die-cutting method for manufacturing self-adhesive labels, and eventually was awarded eighteen patents for his inventions and innovations.

His first orders were for small labels that could be used at functions to identify the participants. The person's name would be written on the label and affixed to his or her clothes. After the function, it could be quickly peeled off without harm to the fabric. Avery later developed other products for advertising and identification, and during World War II entered into contracts with the U.S. government for a broad spectrum of his quick-release and other products.

The company grew rapidly and extended into Europe, Scandinavia, and the United Kingdom through licensing agreements, joint ventures, and acquisitions.[12] It launched a successful initial public offering and was listed on the New York Stock Exchange.

Although Frost came to represent Avery in a wide range of matters, the two men first met in connection with a personal estate. In the early 1960s, Avery lost his wife to a brain tumor. During the probate and tax proceedings following her death, problems arose with the Internal Revenue Service, and Frost was asked to become Avery's new personal legal counsel to resolve these issues and to serve as counsel for the estate of Avery's late wife.[13] By this time, Avery already had become very wealthy and needed legal advice separate and apart from the estate matter. Frost became a trusted legal advisor and close friend of Avery's, and in 1966 joined the Avery Board of Directors.[14]

In retrospect, Avery's success had a remarkable provenance. His company grew into a wildly successful business that today sells a host of office supplies, ranging from the self-adhesive postage stamp, to name tags, to the logos affixed to commercial airplanes via a resilient form of adhesive material that first was developed by Avery.

As the years went by, the Avery Company merged with a leading office products company headquartered on the East Coast called the Dennison Company. The resulting company was Avery Dennison.

From the earliest days that Frost was involved with him, Avery was interested in expanding his company around the world. During Frost's tenure as a director of Avery Dennison, the company gradually increased its presence outside of the United States to a point where a majority of its revenues and profits were derived from overseas operations. Frost thus was closely involved with this global expansion and traveled extensively for the company throughout the world, even after retiring from Gibson, Dunn & Crutcher.

The company board was closely acquainted with all aspects of the company's operations and to this end, the board members traveled throughout the United States and overseas, examining the various operations and facilities and meeting with the local leaders at both business and social functions. Avery believed in "management by walking around," and Frost recalls how his on-site visits created high morale in the local operations, personalized the company's management to its employees, and proved highly educational for senior management and the board. Frost was impressed by the look of pride on the faces of Avery employees, particularly the senior employees, when they met Avery in person, and Avery asked them about their work and lives.

By the time of his death, Avery had become one of the leading citizens of Southern California, widely known for his big heart, his humility, and his community participation. Avery also made good on his promise to "do good wholesale." He was a major benefactor at Cal-Tech and various other charities and became one of Southern California's most generous and beloved philanthropists.

Avery's example of invention, entrepreneurial genius, and philanthropic virtue left a profound mark on Frost. As a manager, Frost sought to emulate Avery's hands-on "walk about" style. As a businessman, Frost tried his own hand at entrepreneurial business ventures. Also following Avery's lead, Frost began to direct a portion of his own wealth to support academic scholarship programs and other charitable ends throughout the American West. He came to embrace the Avery philosophy of first growing one's personal capacity—financial and otherwise—in order to later do greater good "wholesale."[15] In sum, Avery shaped Frost in multiple ways, and the two remained close friends until Avery's death. On several occasions, Frost was asked to introduce Avery at events where he was honored for his many contributions. Frost delighted in making these introductions, often injecting great humor by reciting various "Stanisms"[16]—aphorisms that were Avery's own. This was a client Frost not only admired, but whom he respected deeply and came to love.

Ralph Parsons, Parsons Company

Another influential client in Frost's early years was Ralph Parsons. Frost's start in representing Parsons, the Parsons Company, and its multisubsidiaries ("Parsons") occurred in the 1960s on a tax matter. He was asked by Parsons's outside auditors, Price Waterhouse, if he would be willing to be interviewed by Parsons as Parsons's new outside legal counsel. The original referral came from William Miller, who was then the top Los Angeles tax partner for Price Waterhouse.[17]

The change of auditors and outside legal counsel for Parsons was brought about by a serious dispute with the Internal Revenue Service concerning the worldwide operations of Parsons and the allocation of profits and losses between Parsons's U.S. parent company and its many overseas subsidiaries. This dispute had gone beyond the agent level, and the total amount of deficiencies proposed was large. In effect, the IRS wanted to reallocate all profits to the American parent. These proposed deficiencies extended over many years and involved numerous complex issues under the Internal Revenue Code.

Over the next several years, these issues were resolved to the benefit of Parsons. Parsons then asked Frost to become a director of the parent company, in which post Frost served for the next thirty years. Through Frost's connection to the company's global operations, Frost traveled the world and saw many extraordinary projects in their early stages.

Parsons was in the engineering and construction business, which historically specialized in nuclear power and oil and gas refineries. It originally was owned 100 percent by Ralph Parsons.[18]

Ralph Parsons was a big personality who cut a wide swath in Southern California and beyond. Although he was tremendous at acquiring business, he relied heavily on his chief officers to carry out the marketing function after the initial approach had been made.

A graduate of the Pratt Institute of Technology, which specialized in naval architecture, Parsons loved yachts. At the time Frost became outside legal counsel, Parsons owned a 165-foot yacht—the *Argo*—which was berthed in San Pedro. Parsons used the *Argo* frequently for lavish customer and employee entertainment outings. A typical use was an evening cruise to Avalon Bay, Catalina Island, with a sumptuous buffet, live music, and a crew of about twenty.

Once at Avalon Bay, the passengers would disembark to walk down to the famous Pavilion, and then return to the *Argo* for a boisterous trip home.[19]

The *Argo* ferried many luminaries during its day. Frost recalls one memorable occasion in 1963, when the internationally celebrated Emperor Haile Selassie of Ethiopia was visiting the United States. After a visit to the White House, the emperor was a guest on the *Argo*, along with his entourage and several members of his cabinet.

Parsons's connection to the emperor was a concession to mine for potash in the Eritrea part of the kingdom, near the Red Sea. The emperor's visit aboard the *Argo* was treated by Parsons, and also by the federal and local governments, as a state occasion. Fireboats accompanied the yacht out of the harbor with their typical salutes.[20]

Following this occasion, Frost was sent to Addis Ababa, the capital of Ethiopia, to work on various legal details concerning the mining concession.[21] Frost was asked to meet with the emperor at his palace at Addis—a unique African palace, with black lions in gilded cages outside the entrance. Frost was treated to a review of the emperor's cavalry, who were mounted on stunningly beautiful Arabian horses.

During the 1970s and '80s, Parsons received numerous major contracts in Saudi Arabia that were almost breathtaking in their challenges. The Saudi government decided that a new city (Yanbu) was to be built on the Red Sea as the terminus of an oil pipeline from the major Saudi oil fields in the eastern part of the kingdom, as security from an attack on Riyadh and the eastern provinces of the kingdom. A huge new refinery at Yanbu was being constructed by Parsons and a new government airport also was built by Parsons at nearby Jedda, the gateway of pilgrims to Mecca.[22]

Frost was sent to Saudi Arabia several times during the construction of these two structures with General Bill Leonhard, then CEO of Parsons. When the refinery at Yanbu—the largest in the world—was about to begin operation, the city of Yanbu was under construction. Frost recalls a trip during the Hajj when Leonhard and Frost entered the airport building and found it occupied by thousands of pilgrims waiting for the next step in their trip to Mecca. Security, needless to say, was very tight.

Another Parsons project in the area was the building of a second palace for the king. This one was perched on a site above the Red Sea, just south of Yanbu. Although it had not yet been completed, Frost and Leonhard were allowed to walk through this enormous and beautiful site.

Before Parsons's death, the company held a public offering of stock in order to raise working capital and be listed on the American Stock Exchange. Even after this public offering, however, Parsons still owned approximately 60 percent of the outstanding voting stock. During his later years, Parsons stated to Frost that he wanted his employees to own the company stock. He also wanted to create a Parsons Foundation.

Both of his wishes were fulfilled. The foundation was funded at the time of Parson's death and is today one of the major foundations in Southern California. The employee ownership of company stock was accomplished after his death, through a complicated series of transactions in which an Employee Stock Option Trust was created. In due course the trust acquired the interest of all of the public stockholders, the company was delisted from the American Stock Exchange, and it became again a private company, now owned by the employees.

All of these transactions involved difficult legal and valuation issues, and appraisers, accountants, lawyers, and investment bankers were involved at every step. Litigation nevertheless arose against the company and its officers and directors after the transactions were completed. This entailed second-guessing the valuation, accounting, and legal issues. This litigation went on for several years, but finally was resolved with a victory by summary judgment for Parsons and its directors and officers, which was upheld on appeal.

Sam Mosher, Signal Oil Company

The last client whom Frost regards as among his most memorable was the California oil tycoon Sam Mosher. Mosher struck oil on Signal Hill in the 1920s, one of several sizable deposits discovered in Southern California during this period of development.[23] Soon, the Signal Hill area was littered with drilling rigs and active oil wells.

Mosher formed the Signal Company, which became a public company listed on the New York Stock Exchange. The name of the company changed to the Signal Companies when it began using surplus funds to diversify into a broad range of other businesses.

In the 1960s Frost became personal counsel for Mosher. During this representation, tensions arose between Mosher and Forest Shumway and the Signal Companies. In his later years, Mosher had selected his nephew, Forest Shumway, a graduate of Stanford Law School and an ex-marine, to be his chief operating officer. Eventually Shumway became president. Friction developed between Shumway and Mosher as to various legal and business issues. These issues were resolved by, among other things, the election of Frost, as Mosher's representative, to the Board of the Signal Companies. When Mosher died, Frost and Gibson Dunn became involved in litigation involving his estate.

The complicated and contentious Mosher legal affairs reinforced for Frost the vital importance of sophisticated estate planning. Vast wealth and complex business arrangements make advance planning particularly crucial, because estate challenges are almost inevitable when financial stakes are this high. The clearheaded guidance of counsel early on is a bulwark against the undermining of a client's true intentions and lifetime of hard work, not to mention the fracturing of a family's goodwill and cohesion. Frost's role here, as in other cases, was to be that bulwark.

Other Clients, Other Lessons

Frost's long and distinguished career brought him into contact with numerous other renowned figures, including the late Walt Disney; the Wrigley heiress, Ada E. Wrigley; the founder of Honda Motor Company; the head of North American Aviation; and Richard M. Nixon. Through his association with the Signal Company Board he also met Belton ("B") Kleberg Johnson, one of the principal owners of the King Ranch—an enormous landholding in southern Texas. Frost became counsel for "B" Johnson, and on one matter for King Ranch, at one time the largest producer of natural gas in the United States.[24]

Other notable engagements included work for the California estate of Howard Hughes, after Hughes's death; a major merger and acquisitions program for Purex; and director positions on several major corporate and not-for-profit boards. Through these connections—as well as through his community service—Frost again and again made contacts that led to important business for the firm.

Frost also forged many friendships through his business contacts. One of his dearest friends is Dr. Peter Bing, son of Leo Bing, a New York real estate baron. Frost met Leo Bing and Peter Bing in Elmo Conley's office, when Frost was a young lawyer. Later Frost and Peter Bing served together on the Times Mirror and UCLA Medical Center Oversight boards. The two men also became cofounders of the Music Center Foundation and protégés of Dorothy Chandler, and remain close colleagues to this day.[25]

Frost also represented Walt Disney. Herb Sturdy, Disney's personal attorney, assigned Frost to handle IRS matters for the famous producer/director, and Frost became the only Gibson Dunn colleague besides Sturdy who met with Disney one-on-one. Indeed, Disney himself once escorted Frost through the Disney properties shortly before the opening of the visionary new theme park, Disneyland. Frost recalls Disney's close attention to detail, and how Disney stooped to pick up an item of debris as they traversed the grounds together.

Another well-known client was Walter Knott, Founder of Knott's Berry Farm. Knott became a client and close friend of Frost's before his business began to boom. In his youth, Knott had been a mineral prospector, among other things, and explored the mountains near San Bernardino, where there was a minor gold and silver deposit. Later, Knott added small-crop farming to his ventures and bought a piece of a farm in Orange County, in what is now Anaheim. He was an inventive person, who crossbred berries and created the now famous boysenberry.

Knott and his wife opened a small restaurant on the road going past their farm, which was the main route in Frost's youth from Pasadena and the east part of Los Angeles to the beaches in Orange County. The restaurant featured what Frost describes as "the best homemade fried chicken in the world," and various fruit pies, including Mrs. Knott's famous boysenberry pie. Frost recalls with a broad smile that "*Everyone* stopped over to eat at Knott's Berry Farm, including the Frosts!"

By the early 1960s, Frost had become Knott's personal lawyer and the lawyer for his businesses. One day, Knott asked Frost to meet him at a motel on Interstate 10, not far from San Bernardino. Knott had bought land in the San Bernardino Mountains, where Knott once mined, and had donated this land to the county for use as a park. On the land were old open and tunnel mines.

Knott converted the area into a museum of the old mining days with panoramas of how people lived and worked in mining camps that included life-sized figures, old mining equipment, and tracks. Knott had summoned Frost to the location to give Frost a personal tour of the new park, complete with stories of Knott's life as a miner in the old days. Frost remembers this as "a great day."

Finally, Frost became friends with Steve Brill, the flamboyant founder of *The American Lawyer*. Frost attended a dinner with Brill, during which Brill received a wire from the head of *Time* magazine, angrily denouncing Brill for a piece he had written about a libel matter involving *Time* and Ariel Sharon. Frost recalls that Brill calmly continued his meal after the wire, seemingly untroubled by the threat of legal retaliation in this famous case. At Brill's request, Frost often spoke at *American Lawyer* symposiums throughout the country on law firm management matters.

✦ ✦ ✦

Each of these prominent clients and relationships afforded Frost with an ever-expanding circle of acquaintances and friends. They also helped Frost mature as a leader and future manager of his own increasingly complex business enterprise—a now global law firm. Decisions about compensation structures, identity, business strategies, outreach, office locations and overhead, technological advances, and a host of other issues during 1962 to 1986 were, at the heart, business decisions. Knowing how to handle these complex management challenges was not taught in any law school—not then, and not now. Like the lawyer-managers before him, Frost had to learn on the ground. He benefited from having some of the California business world's most successful and canny business leaders as his mentors. As their lawyer, board member, and friend, Frost soaked up information and drew insights from their industries, their strategies, their lives, their philosophies, their triumphs, and their failures. Not one moment, not one client relationship, ever was wasted on this ambitious and inquisitive man.

✦ ✦ ✦

CHAPTER SIX

The Arc of a Law Firm Leader
From Young Turk to Senior Statesman

D ecember of 1961 was a watershed moment for Frost and the firm. Herbert Sturdy, who had led the firm as "first among equals" for decades, called the thirty-nine-year-old lawyer into his office and told him that there soon would be three new senior partners, effective January 1, 1962: William French Smith, future U.S. attorney general; Julian Von Kalinowski; and F. Daniel Frost. Frost was the youngest of the three, and the youngest ever—before or since—to make it to this final rung in the firm's hierarchy. The decision to elevate these men was made by the senior partners at a time of significant change for Los Angeles, for the firm, and for the legal profession as a whole. To fully appreciate the evolution of Gibson, Dunn, & Crutcher thereafter requires a step backward to review the challenges facing the firm and Sturdy in the postwar era.

The Sturdy Years

Gibson Dunn was still one of the most significant law firms in the region in 1962, but its continued influence was in some doubt. It had grown to sixty-four lawyers, thirty-two of whom were partners and only eight of whom were senior partners. It had a gross annual income of $3.8 million. But by all accounts, it had lost some momentum in the early 1950s as several of its most prominent senior lawyers fell ill, retired, or passed away. The senior attorney Homer Crotty no longer was as active as he once was; Elmo Conley and Stuart Lapp had died; Stuart Neary was in poor health; and others, such as Jack McFarland, had retired or left the firm. Herb Sturdy is widely credited with holding the firm together during this uncertain time, as other leading California firms—most notably the venerable O'Melveny & Myers—threatened to overtake Gibson Dunn in regional influence and stature.

Aptly named, Herb Sturdy provided continuity and ballast during this time of transition from the 1950s until his premature death in January of 1969. He was a brilliant person, dedicated to the firm and willing to assume the burdens of management without complaint. But he also was old school in his management practices, and resistant to some of the powerful demographic changes caused by the dynamics of that era of professional transformation. By 1962, the need for changes in the firm's office management policies was palpable.

Sturdy's fellow senior partners were even more resistant to the needed changes in management. When Sturdy implemented time sheets and sought to impose greater control over their billing practices, many of his senior colleagues balked at the innovation, and some groused that the firm was losing its identity as a profession and becoming "a business." The tradition-bound Norm Sterry, in particular, was resistant to recording his time in the new ways Sturdy requested.

This request for greater lawyer accountability for billing and profitability, and the resistance to it by senior lawyers, were common occurences throughout the profession during this time. Firm management practices nationwide were shifting away from the traditional "family/business lawyer" model to a modernized version of the lawyer as a business manager, as well as practitioner. The changes and resistance to these shifts thus were not unique to Gibson, Dunn & Crutcher. Nor did the process of change or resistance to it end in the 1960s. (Senior lawyers in 2011 still chafe at some of the changes of the 1980s, and some remain skeptical about strategies that managers implemented in order to boost the firm's profits and maintain a competitive edge.)

But the older insistence that "law is a profession not a business" all but disappeared after the Sturdy era and in many respects was always more myth than fact. Most lawyers view the Sturdy era as a more genteel and slower-paced time for the profession than the ones that followed; yet few of them who practiced law then romanticize law firm life before the 1960s and '70s. Lawyers of the Sturdy era too worked hard and devoted much of themselves to their practice. Many of them died relatively young, even before the 24/7 service and 2,200-billable-hour years of the 1990s. Moreover, the anti-competitive and outright discriminatory practices that defined elite firms in earlier times belie claims that these were, in every respect, the "good old days" of the profession. That is, the Sturdy era precipitated changes that were necessary and undeniably positive, as well as ones that were necessary and controversial.

One critical change that followed the Sturdy era was the advent of the more complex, internal management structures. The management committees, law school recruitment programs, and other internal structures that today are de rigueur at Gibson Dunn and other major firms did not yet exist. For example, Sturdy became the firm's de facto managing partner by default, rather than by being elected through a formal process. He was chosen because he was a highly self-disciplined attorney who was willing to do the demanding and often thankless work of managing colleagues. But he was neither groomed for the post nor trained for its growing complexities.

Working alongside Sturdy was Corinne McCallum, who both protected Sturdy and helped him to maintain his tight managerial control—including control of the financial records of the firm. Together, they were a formidable, secretive team. Indeed, when Frost became a senior partner, the firm's internal financial records still were a mystery to other senior partners and held close to Sturdy's vest alone.

Although Sturdy steered the firm ably enough to get it through the post–World War II era intact, he clearly missed opportunities, in part because of his noncollaborative managerial style. He was a naturally reserved person who lacked community and business outreach instincts. The result was that other firms captured the emerging film and television industry business, as well as the lucrative corporate work for the aerospace companies that became a powerful component in the California economy during World War II. Gibson Dunn did handle the labor relations work of the aerospace industry—a coup attributable to Stuart Neary and Elmo Conley. But other opportunities slipped through the firm's fingers because Sturdy and other firm lawyers were not as aggressive about attracting new clients as they might have been, or as other lawyers of the time were willing to be. By the early 1960s, a new day was dawning for all of the major California firms, and the dominance of O'Melveny & Myers, along with an atmosphere of increased competition for business more generally, were becoming serious threats to Gibson Dunn.

The firm also suffered from internal factionalism. Sturdy's brother Fred—not as brilliant or as successful a lawyer as his brother—nevertheless was promoted to senior partner ahead of other, likely more deserving, colleagues. This move inspired friction among the more senior lawyers and threatened to compromise the firm's hallmark cohesion.

Another notable problem was the absence of a formal retirement program—coupled with improved life spans of the older lawyers. This meant that the tensions between the prewar generation of leaders and the emerging leaders were difficult to ease. Whenever turnover at the top is low, and memories for grievances are long and hard, a workplace atmosphere sours. When these internal grievances also involve family relations and create the appearance or reality that nepotism trumps merit, these problems can lead to defections or even dissolution. By 1962, the need for changes at many levels was painfully apparent to Frost, and to many of his colleagues.

Yet, Gibson Dunn clearly owes an enormous debt to Sturdy—a debt that Frost and other leaders who followed Sturdy acknowledge. Most notably, it was Herb Sturdy who requested that Frost institute an overseas practice in Europe and the United Kingdom for the firm and who, in 1967, assigned young Frost to open an office in Paris. By this time, several major New York firms already had Paris offices—some of which had opened as early as the 1920s—and Sturdy believed that establishing a presence in Paris would enhance the firm's reputation and influence.[1]

Herb Sturdy also was the first to hire a professional administrator—Herb Schwab—to assist in managing the growing firm's internal affairs. And it was Herb Sturdy who personally oversaw the establishment of the Beverly Hills office of the law firm, and its expansion on Spring Street in Los Angeles.

Above all, and despite all of the issues and festering conflicts within the firm during his time as manager, Sturdy was a steadying force. He recognized the need for change and enabled a bloodless coup to facilitate the transformations that he knew he could not effect personally. His decision to relinquish the reins to others who had very different management instincts than his own likely was a conscious ploy, because once the three "young turks" came on board, Sturdy was surprisingly willing to let them take charge. He complied when they pushed for access to the firm's financial records and other changes that were necessary to maintain Gibson, Dunn's status as a leading firm of the future, not merely one that had shone brightly in the past. In short, he knew when his own time had passed, and the rising generation's turn had come—the mark of an uncommonly mature and wise leader.

Beyond Herbert Sturdy: The Frost Era

When Sturdy passed the reins in 1962, the firm was at a crossroads. Two of the most pressing changes were a new work ethic and greater lawyer accountability for profitability. In turning to Frost—as well as to Smith and Von Kalinowski—Sturdy sent an unambiguous signal to others who aspired to become senior partners thereafter about both aspects of a lawyer's responsibility to the firm. Frost already was billing well over 2,000 hours a year. He was exceptionally active in the Los Angeles community, and was well respected as a tax lawyer, ambitious, self-confident, and above all—hard working. He also was strong-minded, and unwilling to be a senior partner in name only. Indeed, Frost and his other recently promoted colleagues immediately insisted on seeing the firm's financial statements—something that Sturdy's assistant, Corinne McCallum, first refused to permit. They went to Sturdy directly, pushed, and prevailed. As they recall, the meeting was tense but cordial, and produced the result they sought. For perhaps the first time, these records were open to, and reviewed by, someone other than Herb Sturdy and his inner administrative team. This was the beginning of an internal revolution of management, and greater accountability in individual and productivity.

The firm thereafter began to create new committee structures, and—most important—adopted a retirement program for senior lawyers and their surviving spouses. Frost later observed that when he was in his late thirties, the firm had no living partner over sixty-five. They "worked hard, some drank hard, and many died young." But as life expectancies grew, it became more important to develop a formal plan of succession and retirement that also respected the firm's promise that its senior lawyers would be taken care of. In response, the firm set an ordinary retirement age of sixty-eight, staged in during the transition years, and adopted a rule that after age sixty-five, senior partners were rotated off the Executive Committee, would begin process of reduced shares, and would step down. No longer was a partner assured of position and power that endured beyond his or her most productive years. The firm would take care of the senior lawyers and their families financially, but not be unduly weighted down by an older, less agile generation in its future-oriented decision-making.

The firm also adopted quite strict anti-nepotism rules at this time—to avoid another Fred/Herb Sturdy conflict. In all of this, Frost and his young colleagues sought to institutionalize more certain methods for transitions in authority, while respecting the senior colleagues' contributions. In so doing, they created an enduring expectation of, and structures for, perpetual renewal.

In establishing the new culture for the firm, Frost believed it was crucial that one could rise to leadership and have an impact on the firm's direction without "waiting for the death of a senior partner." This, too, was a key shift in philosophy—one that may well have saved the firm from a decline from which it might never have recovered.

The "senior partner" tier was abandoned by 1970, and a Financial Management Committee—which Frost chaired—was created. All partners were afforded access to financial records, and transparency about finances became the new norm. The old guard was, in effect, dispossessed of power. But as stated above, Sturdy himself recognized both that these changes were necessary and that he was not the person to effect them. He also had developed serious health problems, which resulted in his early death in 1969.

Sturdy was succeeded by Van Niven, who also died at an early age and never was the commanding presence that Sturdy was. The reins then formally passed to Frost, who became the first real successor to Sturdy in terms of strong leadership. Frost held the reins until 1986, when Norman Barker took the helm.[2]

Perhaps the most important changes in internal structure of the firm after 1962 were the creation of a long-range planning committee and a small, agile management committee. The latter was composed initially of Frost, William French Smith, and Francis M. Wheat, who later became commissioner of the Securities and Exchange Commission. The members and the chair of the committee—functionally the managing partner—were chosen by the Long-Range Management Committee. The firm's first elected managing partner was Frost, after other senior partners decided that the firm should formally adopt the managing partner model. Partners on the Long-Range Planning Committee who themselves were not candidates for the position decided, first, who would be on the new management committee and, second, who would chair it. In other words, a handful of the firm's partners decided who would become the managing partner, and by 1978 the management group was a small one selected for their skill at business planning. The elected chair of this elite team was Frost.

Although the Long-Range Planning Committee eventually disappeared, matters of succession continue to be determined by a small committee, not by the firm's members as a whole. The outgoing managing partner exercises tremendous control over the decision about his or her successor because he or she appoints the committee that makes the ultimate decision. This aspect of succession was initiated by Frost. None of the members of that committee can themselves be candidates for the job. Finally, the managing partner serves a five-year term, which is renewable.

The receding generation correctly grasped that for the law firm to survive and thrive, it was necessary to relinquish power and let the ascending generation have its turn at the wheel. Frost was the

PHOTO ALBUM

✦ ✦ ✦

Frost and his wife, Sue, in the backyard of their Tucson home.

(ABOVE) Frost Scholar Wynona Peters checks the scoreboard in a Salpointe tournament victory. Wynona is still a Frost Scholar and is now a senior at the University of San Diego. *Photo courtesy of the Arizona Daily Star.*

(UPPER RIGHT) Dinner at Arizona Inn honoring "Sister Jackie" Koenig, now deceased, for her many years as the head and heart of San Xavier Mission School, and two of her graduates, then Frost Scholars at Salpointe Catholic High School, Wynona Peters and Nadia Negrette. Frost believes Sister Jackie "walks with God."

(LOWER RIGHT) Frost and Frost Scholar Wynona Peters at Salpointe Catholic High School.

See Appendix C for complete Arizona Daily Star article on Wynona Peters.

Frost's gift to the city of Kennewick of a 55,000-square-foot building encompassing more than seven acres was designated by the city as the "Dan Frost Municipal Services Campus." *Photo courtesy of Mark Roberts Photography.*

R El Jefe

ATBA Fall Sales Stakes (Colts & Geldings Division)

F. Daniel & S. Fifer Frost, Owners
David Van Winkle, Trainer
Juan Rivera, Up
6 Furlongs 1:09.44   October 17, 2009

Purse $76,928.00
Espresso Springs (2nd)
De Sica (3rd)
$7.40 $3.20 $2.60

For many years Frost has had a small racing stable. His horse R El Jefe won the Arizona two-year-old championship in 2009. *Photo courtesy of Coady Photography.*

One of Frost's most cherished awards is the Centennial Medal from the University of Arizona, presented to the most outstanding 100 graduates (out of 180,000) in the history of the university at the centennial graduation ceremony in 1989.

Claremont University Center

Board of Fellows

January 16, 1978

Resolution of Appreciation

F. Daniel Frost

F. Daniel Frost has provided valued service to Claremont
University Center since his election to the Board of Fellows
ten years ago.

For five of those years he made an important contribution
to the work of the Committee on Nominations, and chaired
this committee in 1975-76. From 1969 to 1975 he was
Vice-Chairman of the Board of Fellows and from 1971 to 1975
he served as a member and then as Chairman of the Executive
Committee. He also served for a period of three years as
a member of the Committee on the Graduate School.

Daniel Frost was one of the architects of the Constitution
adopted by the Board of Fellows in 1976. His wise counsel
during the period of reorganization as well as his contribution
to the ongoing work of the Board is acknowledged with deep
appreciation by his fellow members.

**Resolution of Appreciation from Claremont University Center
(Claremont, California) for Frost's services on that board.**

Award given to Frost by the Los Angeles Bar Association Taxation Section for distinguished lifetime service to the Tax Bar. Frost is a former chairman of the Tax Section.

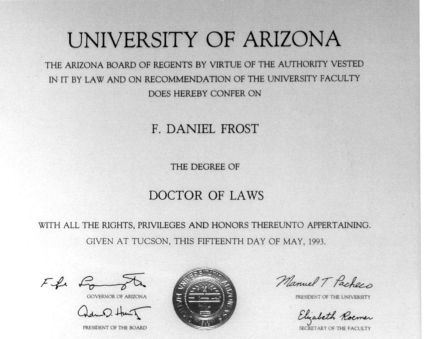

UNIVERSITY OF ARIZONA

THE ARIZONA BOARD OF REGENTS BY VIRTUE OF THE AUTHORITY VESTED
IN IT BY LAW AND ON RECOMMENDATION OF THE UNIVERSITY FACULTY
DOES HEREBY CONFER ON

F. DANIEL FROST

THE DEGREE OF

DOCTOR OF LAWS

WITH ALL THE RIGHTS, PRIVILEGES AND HONORS THEREUNTO APPERTAINING.
GIVEN AT TUCSON, THIS FIFTEENTH DAY OF MAY, 1993.

GOVERNOR OF ARIZONA

PRESIDENT OF THE BOARD

PRESIDENT OF THE UNIVERSITY

SECRETARY OF THE FACULTY

At the University of Arizona graduation ceremony in May 1991, Frost
was awarded an honorary Doctor of Laws.

Original bronze sculpture presented to Frost at his retirement from Parsons Board of Directors, inscribed "To Dan Frost, our friend and trusted advisor whose leadership, strength and wisdom helped forge Parsons into one of the premier engineering and construction organizations in the world. We are forever grateful."

This sculpture, presented to Frost on his retirement from the Times Mirror Company Board in 1992, is a replica of the eagle in the lobby of Times Mirror honoring General Otis, founder of the company.

This Kohima Memorial, located at the Imperial War Museum, Duxford, UK, has the insignia of the Burma Star Association (of which Frost is a member) and the moving inscription "When you go home tell them of us and say 'For your tomorrow, we gave our today.'"

Taken in 1945 on the China/Tibet border prior to a mission into Tibet
to investigate the fate of a B-29 and its crew lost on a flight from India
to China. Shown are high-ranking Chinese military and governmental
officials who provided the base for the operation.

A flight over "the Hump" (Himalayas) from Allied air bases in Assam, India, to Kunming and other destinations in China to supply Chinese and U.S. forces in their military action against Japan.

beneficiary of this insight, carried it forward, and progressed out of his own post as managing partner before his term elapsed. In other words, he believed in renewal even when it meant that his own time as manager should end. Of course, such transitions are always bittersweet, even when they are foreseen, accepted, or self-initiated.

Leadership transitions also inevitably reflect the times in which they occur, and the new leaders often err on the side of correcting for whatever appeared to them to be the greatest weaknesses of the former generation. So it was with the "young turk" revolution.

The proliferation of committees, the rapid democratization of management, and the drive to managerial transparency in 1962 to 1979 were both a response to more general forces within the legal profession and to the specific idiosyncrasies of Sturdy's personal management style. The innovations effected by the "turks" inevitably reflected the arrogance of youth, whose early, heady ideas about management often need the leavening of actual leadership experience. Things always look different from outside of management than they appear from inside. When Frost experienced firsthand from the panoptic vantage point of management the intense pressures of competition, the complications of personnel sensitivities, the economic headaches, and the other challenges of running a major business—some of which were best handled quietly and behind closed doors, rather than aired generally with all members of the firm—he later opted for oligarchy rather than true democracy.

In fairly short order, Frost thus learned a central lesson of leadership—leading does not always mean co-deciding. By the late 1970s, he steered the firm back to a far more centralized governance model. Although it still included transparency and consultation—in 1981 the firm created an Advisory Committee to provide input to the powerful Management Committee—the membership was selective, and the issues on which they were consulted were identified by the Management Committee itself.

The rapid, almost staggering growth of the firm made this greater centralization of management nearly essential. As Frost later observed, by the 1980s the firm—or, at the least, its more senior partners—recognized that "you cannot run a large business by committee." And the firm had indeed become a large business—in October of 1984 it was the sixth largest firm in the United States. In significant respects, the managing partner and inner team took control of nearly all administrative affairs, in order to afford the lawyers more time to practice law, rather than spend excessive amounts of time on internal governance.

Finding the proper balance between diffusion and centralization, between consultation and independent leadership, and between transparency and confidentiality, is a delicate task for anyone in a leadership position. It depends not only on the size and composition of an organization, but also on its culture, its context, and—above all—on the judgment and wisdom of its leaders. Nobody else has—or often should have—all of the information necessary to make every strategic decision, and nobody else occupies the bird's-eye perch from which to assess the radical consequences of organizational movements.

But effective leaders also must profit from others' insights, avoid the pitfall of isolated thinking, make clear for colleagues the firm's direction, and inspire confidence. Indeed, the morale of team members is the greatest intangible factor in any human organization's ability to invent and prosper. Effective leaders not only must be willing and able to shoulder adversity for others and must weather and counteract the inevitable pressures and tempests that come with any business—indeed, with any public or private endeavor—they also must give all members of the organization a sense of participation and ownership. As one of the senior partners, as a member of the key committees, and especially as managing partner, Frost therefore came to appreciate the need to carry many things on his broad shoulders alone, just as Herb Sturdy had. At the same time, he understood that the consequences of his leadership decisions would be generally experienced by members of the firm—even if many of the challenges remained hidden from public view. Finally, Frost knew that his actions on behalf of the whole would affect its constituents and be judged by them in time, just as he and his colleagues had been affected by and had judged his predecessors' actions.

"One Firm, One Culture": One Leader

Above all, Frost understood that an effective leader never can delegate away the articulation of the firm's strategy. Colleagues can be consulted, retreats convened, and outside specialists deployed to assist in the process. "Mission Statements" can be co-created, and must match, as well as advance, the actual people and practices of a given institution in order to be practical, viable, attainable. But the job of expressing these values coherently, and of assuring that they in fact are advanced at every level of decision making, depends upon the central leadership of an organization. This general rule applies to law firms, no less than to other professions or other institutions.

For Gibson, Dunn & Crutcher during the 1970s to late 1980s, the task of strategy articulation fell to Frost. He possessed a clear sense of the firm's essential identity—one that he worked tirelessly to maintain throughout the turbulent decades when he served as a senior partner and as managing partner. He also thought about the firm's identity daily, and he expressed it convincingly and charismatically to his fellow lawyers.

To assure that all understood the mission, Frost inaugurated in 1980 an annual meeting at which he outlined for members the elements of his vision. The speeches he delivered at this annual gathering of the firm's lawyers are the best windows into Frost's strategic thinking during these years. In these addresses, Frost detailed his philosophy, outlined his financial and strategic planning, and made transparent to his colleagues the nature of their competition and how the firm intended to meet the challenges of the times. The text of the Frost speeches thus is an indispensable part of Gibson, Dunn & Crutcher's history.[3]

Frost's vision also was reinforced in the firm's self-descriptive documents, which became highly visible, shared understandings of what it meant to be a Gibson, Dunn & Crutcher lawyer, versus a lawyer at any other top-tier firm that named "excellence" as a central value. Frost created the basic creed from which all the firm's benchmarks and strategic planning—also Frost trademarks—proceeded thereafter.

Western Character

First—and in keeping with his personal identity—Frost emphasized the western character of Gibson, Dunn & Crutcher. To Frost, "western" did not mean provincial or even regional per se; it meant "old in years but young in nature." In the West, Gibson, Dunn & Crutcher already was a senior firm, founded when fewer than 120,000 people lived in Los Angeles. But it was still emerging and young in other respects. Frost elaborated on this in his address to the firm at the 1982 annual meeting:

> The fact that the firm is old means that it has traditional ties to and pride in the past. By the term "Western," I mean that the firm is informal and not stratified. By young in nature I mean that it is aggressive, opportunistic, and hard working. The term "growing" means opportunity and mobility. The fact that we have moved from a regional to a national and international firm and practice sophisticated law means that we are in the forefront of the legal practice.

His own experience with the firm, beginning in his library days through the Sturdy era and beyond taught Frost the importance of camaraderie to cohesion. The intimacy of the early partnership meetings, and even the personal touch of recognizing partner birthdays, made a deep impression on him. He understood, however, that the informality and enviable collegiality of this western firm would be difficult to maintain as the firm took root in other cities, other countries. As he continued, in this same firm address,

> We must constantly work at keeping our sense of collegiality that we have always had. We must seek to have our associates fully understand the opportunities that are available to them because of the growth of the firm. This only occurs through communication.

This concern, among other reasons, is why Frost created the annual state-of-the firm address: it helped forge coherence and a shared identity. Frost also traveled ceaselessly, and made every effort to visit the firm's many offices across the country and overseas. He hosted breakfasts, lunches, and dinners with his colleagues in other places. These acts reflected his understanding that with growth came the challenge of "being able to maintain the culture, the spirit, the congeniality" of the firm to which he had devoted so much of his career, his time, his life.

By all accounts, this sense of culture was preserved, despite the pressures of the increasingly aggressive professional environment. That Frost succeeded in preserving it is evidenced by the following heartfelt letter from his partner Jim Clark, written on the occasion of Frost's retirement:

> During the past dozen years, nothing in my life save my family has shaped it more than our great firm. And no force—human, economic or natural—has so shaped the firm, has so ensured its greatness, as has Dan Frost.
>
> Many, indeed all of us, must and do thank you for what you have done for "the firm." But I most want to express my gratitude and admiration for what you have *not* done, what you have

"managed" to avoid. For, while creating a well-run strategically sound, economically vital enterprise (and not always with the greatest help from your partners) you have not permitted Gibson, Dunn & Crutcher to become an institution, a monolith. I sincerely doubt that anyone else could have assumed, at once, both the firm's prosperity, and its humanity. You leave the management committee with the firm not only strong, but warm, not only large, but living.

According to the current managing partner, Ken Doran, this general commitment to the firm's culture endured. In Doran's words, the "western" character still means "Entrepreneurial, collegial, and (relatively) more casual than Eastern counterparts."

Profitability

A strong sense of community alone does not sustain a firm as a business. Frost grasped that the firm's prosperity also required profitability. In fact, he believed that the *most* important ingredient of the firm's success was its profitability relative to its competitors. He was keenly attuned at all times to the firm's numbers, which he could quote instantly and without reference to notes, calculators, or charts. He was known for his cautious approach to investment, and abhorrence of capital debt. He maintained a skeptical view of economic booms, never forgetting the lessons of the Great Depression. When others chided him for being overly cautious, he simply responded by observing "I worry if I'm *not* worrying." He maintained a combination of wariness about expenditures and a willingness to act decisively when the numbers justified the risks and costs of a new venture. He watched as other firms borrowed to pay their obligations and found themselves unable to pay them when recessions hit. High-profile lateral hires were made by some firms that lacked the profits to support them; still others spent great sums on advertising or on their physical plants, then found themselves unable to make payroll.

Frost sought to avoid all of these traps. Yet he also wanted the best in terms of work product and physical facilities, and he understood that aesthetics influence the public's perception and the members' sense of themselves. He believed both goals could best be achieved if the firm had a "clean balance sheet" and avoided the waste of appearances *over* substance. To maximize average partner income and net income per share was the ultimate measure, to Frost, of whether a particular expenditure was "prudent." Any expansion had to come from earnings and capital assessments. To aid this process, he developed a protocol by which the firm withheld from profit payouts an involuntary "capital contribution" by the lawyers. No interest ever was paid on this "loan." When a lawyer retired, he or she received a full cash return on this withholding, but with no interest. In this and other ways, Frost creatively and cleverly structured finances to offer attorneys handsome compensation and a solid retirement fund, while also assuring a strong foundation to support operations and assure ongoing profitability.

In making these financial plans, Frost relied in part on his exceptional ability to see financial relationships in advance. While managing partner, he once sketched out—again, without the use of a computer or calculator—a prediction of the 1985 budget. His handwritten estimate yielded a net income "available for dividends" of $53.8 million. The financial department—using computers and all other available charts, records, and tools—estimated $45.53 million. The actual figure for the year came in at $54.76 million—Frost was off by only 1.7 percent.

His almost uncanny mathematical instincts, knowledge of all aspects of finances, and tax and accounting expertise enabled Frost to zero in on the true bottom-line of his own firm and to apprehend accurately the financial landscape in which all large law firms then operated. At the same time, however, he clung to an idealized, almost poetic, sense of the firm's character and identity. This was an unusual combination of qualities: visionary and optimistic yet financially astute and coldly realistic. It enabled Frost to imagine and implement a strategic plan that was a compelling and bold blueprint for an exciting future, not a fantasy destined to founder on the shoals of the real world.

The results were simply staggering. Frost was manager of the firm from 1979 to 1986 and remained an active partner until 1988. In less than a decade, as the following chart demonstrates, gross revenues and number of lawyers soared:

	Revenue	Attorneys
1980	43,861,068	240
1981	55,530,089	271
1982	63,647,652	312
1983	78,013,895	342
1984	100,992,021	404
1985	124,971,425	447
1986	156,250,700	521
1987	190,133,436	576
1988	236,947,572	651

It had taken the firm ninety-four years to hit $100 million, and only four more years to reach the $200 million milestone—indeed, to significantly exceed it.

In sum, Frost maintained a lofty vision of a unified and collegial character for the firm, but he coupled it with a "no debt, tight reins, and green eye shades" sense of financial sustainability that worked phenomenally well. He combined tradition with modernity in forging policy. At the same time, he illustrated what is missing in the flatter, three-pocket description of law firm personalities as "finders, minders, or grinders." Great firms need all three types of contributors, but they need a person with the ability to bring out the best of all three—a so-called visionary who will give his colleagues and potential recruits a compelling reason to choose *this* firm, over the hundreds of others vying for the best talent. Frost's answer to the question "Why Gibson, Dunn & Crutcher?" was fourfold: we offer great clients, great colleagues, great culture, and great compensation. Producing all four of these, of course, required smart choices.

Growth

Growth was a critical component of Frost's vision for the firm. Moreover, his growth philosophy was an important example of how his personal characteristics, coupled with his devotion to the firm, guided his most important decisions.

In the 1970s the dominance of New York City's major law firms in corporate law was unrivaled. The best law students from the most elite law schools sought to practice "big law" there—a euphemism for a lucrative practice at a major law firm that represents leading corporations and entrepreneurs, and does sophisticated securities, merger and acquisitions, and corporate restructuring work. The best among the law graduates gravitated to Manhattan —where the epitome of "making it" was a position with firms such as Sullivan and Cromwell; Cravath, Swain & Moore; Cleary, Gottlieb; Shearman & Sterling; or Davis Polk. From there, many of the lawyers catapulted to Goldman Sachs, to the Federal Reserve, to high-profile posts with the federal government, or to other positions of influence and prestige. These lawyers' view of the rest of the nation—of the rest of the world, in fact—was not unlike the famous Saul Steinberg cartoon depicting a New Yorker's view of the world, where Manhattan occupies most of the nation, and the rest of the country appears either as distant colonial outposts, or does not appear at all.

When new economic opportunities arose on the West Coast in the 1960s through 1980s, it hence did not occur to the New York firms that businesses there would not want the superior expertise of a "New York lawyer." The firms sent emissaries to these emerging markets to do reconnaissance, to set up branch offices, and to capture the new industries and the projects to be gained by offering them top-flight legal counsel.

One can easily imagine Frost, sitting in his office in downtown Los Angeles, seeing the early signs of an eastern invasion and thinking to himself: "Not *my* firm, not on *my* watch, not in *my* town." By this time, Frost no longer was a young, relatively untutored student with a lot to learn from East Coast and foreign sophisticates. Nor was the West more generally the relatively parochial place it was in Frost's youth. The California economy was leading the nation and had become a world force, not only a national one, in its own right. Western research universities in California, Washington, Arizona, Texas, and Colorado—public and private—had begun to match and even outstrip many venerable East Coast institutions in the generation of research funding, science and technology advances, and academic prestige. All of this gave Frost individually, as well as Frost as a leader among California's elite law firm culture, the confidence and audacity not only to protect his own turf from eastern invasion, but to head east himself to invade some of their turf.

It needs to be underscored that Frost was competitive—fiercely so. His determination and will to win were formidable, drawn from a daunting combination of physical and mental strength that he brought to every challenge. If a battle were to be fought over California soil, Frost would not sit on the sidelines and let the marauders win easily. He also had tremendous pride, and had a deep personal investment in Gibson, Dunn & Crutcher's name, as well as in its glory. He would not allow that investment to sour. Finally, he had a strong will and strong opinions. As Ken Doran has put it, "Dan is very persuasive. He can convince and cajole, through conviction in his views and by presenting vastly more facts than the people he is trying to persuade." Another observer has said that Frost could be "single-minded and driven, characterized by his legal colleagues as alternately charming and cold—'Dan Frost is more like his name than any man I ever met in the legal profession.'"[4]

Yet Frost also possessed charisma and the personal skills to inspire allegiances—which he drew upon in convincing others in the firm to take the leaps he recommended. As another account states, "Frost the businessman can appear cold, aloof, and rigidly exacting. . . . But with his friends he is extremely outgoing and warm."[5]

Frost considered carefully what others said—if only in private. He knew how, in the words of his law partner Ron Beard, to walk "the very difficult, thin line between being very strong and yet managing to build a consensus and not create a riot."[6] For example, he often followed a strong, even gruff, move with a gracious or self-effacing gesture, which softened opposition and inspired respect among his fellow lawyers. They understood his dedication to the firm and appreciated in particular his almost "grandfatherly" interest in other lawyers, as well as his respect for the firm's history. Gibson Dunn partner William Wegner recalls, in reflecting on Frost's leadership when Wegner still was a novice lawyer, that Frost cared about others' well-being. When Frost introduced Wegner to clients, to office staff, or other lawyers at the firm, he always prefaced the introductions with "and this is our good friend ——," showing respect for one and all. Wegner also remembers a lunch with Frost during his first week at the firm, at which Frost advised Wegner and two other new lawyers to "avoid becoming involved in firm intrigues"; "just concentrate on providing clients with great service and the rest will take care of itself." As Wegner later reflected on his career, he noted, "Dan was absolutely correct. And when I recently celebrated my thirty years with [Gibson Dunn] I found I wanted to reach out to Dan, and thank him. He was a visionary and we owe him a lot." Frost was able to make fellow lawyers feel they were in his care, not merely lines on a roster.

But to outsiders of the firm, Frost was a powerful force with a searing will to prevail and absolute clarity of purpose. One did not want to be on the wrong end of Frost in a debate, in a negotiation, or in a turf battle.

It was no surprise, therefore, that as the eastern invasion gained momentum in late 1981, Gibson, Dunn & Crutcher announced that it would in 1982 open a New York office. Nor was it a surprise that this was to be a full-service office, not a mere "filing branch" of the firm where the principal function of the attorneys was to merely file documents with the Securities and Exchange Commission, or shepherd business from elsewhere through the financial institutions there. In this respect, it became the first non–New York law firm to establish a real base in the city.

Here again, Frost's decision showed both daring and caution. Growth of the firm during his tenure as a managing partner was purposeful, never for its own sake, and always financially sustainable. His description of the growth philosophy, articulated in his last annual address to the firm as managing partner, is worth quoting at length:

> Growth is not good or bad in itself—it depends on the purpose and how it is done. Bad growth is growth just to be the biggest firm without accomplishing anything else. Good growth . . . is the growth occurring for the purpose of upgrading the practice, broadening the client base, expanding into a new specialty, or expanding one's capability in a particular specialty, growth for the purpose of achieving strength and depth in lawyering skills . . . .
>
> And let me make one point very clear. The fact that, in my view, we need to grow at a fairly rapid rate [in 1984] does not mean that we can't change that model in the future . . . . The growth model is not a Ponzi scheme. When a firm in the growth model has achieved its desired size, it might well switch to the no growth mode.

That is, growth was wedded to the Frost hallmark: a sober-minded financial assessment of the risks and an ever vigilant ear to the ground of changing economic forces.

The growth strategy also was directly linked to increased specialization within the legal profession. Frost not only wanted the firm to have the ability to deliver legal services in all of the major industrial and financial areas of the world; he wanted it to have the ability to offer clients highly skilled attorneys in the most sophisticated and specialized areas of the law. To do this, physical expansion was imperative.

Growth also required the immediate infusion of talent and experience, which led the firm to begin more lateral hiring. This departure from the firm's past practice of "growing its own" proved to be a wise innovation.

For example, the decision to open a Denver office was based on assessment of the firm's relative weak presence in the area of oil and gas business and a desire to grow in this specialty. Denver had become a mecca for the natural resource industry and for major companies in the industry to locate their home offices. Gibson, Dunn & Crutcher therefore sent prominent members to head up the Denver office and made a significant lateral hire—Charlie Meyers, former dean of the Stanford Law School—to staff the new site. The Dallas office capitalized on the booming Texas economy and enabled the firm to provide better service to American Airlines, a major client.[7]

This same growth pattern was repeated with each new office. In each case, the firm first outlined a clear idea of why the new location would enable the firm as a whole to diversify and amplify its client portfolio.[8] It then found the right lawyers to make that office a success.

Another distinctive feature of the Frost growth model was that there was one pool of profits. Growth therefore had to increase, not deplete, income per share. No single office, department, or group within the firm could be treated as an independent profit center within the firm. This meant, in Frost's words, that "when one partner prospers, all partners prosper; when one office prospers, all offices prosper." Offices were interdependent as a financial matter, as well as a matter of the "one firm" culture.

Sound and cautious as this strategy was, it was hardly uncontroversial. The opening of a new office inevitably involves cash outlay and risks diffusing the firm's identity, its partner profits, and general control of its structures. Moreover, heading into New York City in particular—the most muscular and established of all American legal markets—struck some of the firm's lawyers and outside observers as more foolish than bold. The many objections to the move were thoughtful ones that could not be taken lightly. And Frost, of all people, seemed an unlikely person to risk failure—or worse, embarrassment—for the firm. He was a cautious businessman—one who even understated potential end-of-year bonuses and then surprised colleagues with upticks, rather than boost the figures early in a year, only to disappoint them. As we have seen, Frost consistently steered the firm away from debt and negotiated financially favorable deals for office space and other facilities enhancement. In one case, he refused to approve an expensive "coved" ceiling feature to the new Los Angeles offices in order to cut $300,000 from the architectural and construction costs, then used the savings to instead invest in a collection of plein air artwork and museum quality photographs that reflected the history of the firm and of California, and that became a valuable showcase collection. In short, Frost was, and ever would be, a child of the Depression, who rimmed his ambition with a wary scan of the horizon, looking for financial risk and even ruin.

Frost also knew that the economic times were less than ideal for a New York expansion. In the early 1980s, the country was steeped in a serious recession. Though the Great Recession of 2007 dwarfed that of the 1980s, this earlier recession was then the worst one since World War II. As is true of the Great Recession, the economic indicators in the early 1980s suggested that the recovery would be slow and possibly incomplete: the real estate and automobile industries were suffering already, and it was hardly clear that either would recover fully. For all markets, including legal ones, these times were tough indeed. It was all the more remarkable, then, that Frost forged ahead and opened the New York office in 1982. Yet this calculated and controversial move paid off in spades—it was Frost's biggest victory as manager.

The office quickly grew, and its good fortune eventually quieted even the skeptics. Frost later described, with considerable pride, visiting the New York office and finding it "stuffed with lawyers," all of whom were using the expensive New York City real estate as efficiently and productively as possible.

This strategic move positioned Gibson Dunn when law firms from across the nation moved in and began raiding top partners from leading California firms. Described as a "legal gold rush,"[9] the late 1980s marked the end of many prominent law firms, in the Darwinian struggle for turf in a lucrative California market. Although signs of change started to surface in the early 1980s, the sharp spike in competition by the closing years of the decade surprised nearly everyone. The booming Pacific Rim economy, the influx of leading financial institutions, and increased foreign investment in the West all made California an irresistible target. Aggressive recruitment of leading lawyers, coupled with dazzling compensation packages and the rush of being wooed, led many partners and associates to defect to other, larger firms. To take but one breathtaking example—New York's Skadden, Arps, Slate, Meagher & Flom established a Los Angeles office in 1983 that ballooned from six to eighty lawyers in only four years. Many midsized firms were swallowed up or utterly drained of marquee talent.

Gibson Dunn was not immune to these pressures, but its smart growth, its long-standing emphasis on culture, and its attention to profitability helped it to defend against suitors. Having established a New York presence signaled that it was willing and able to go toe-to-toe with the most ambitious and voracious national firms. Rather than hunkering down in Los Angeles during this war for talent and clients, the firm had charged the hill—New York City, no less—and had done some raiding of its own along the way.

Of course, the changes Frost authored were not an unmixed blessing. Some firm lawyers were unwilling to sacrifice as much of their personal lives as the new transformation of work culture, billing demands, and structure required. A group of them decided to leave the firm for other settings. These lawyers were not raided by the big firms, or interested in challenging them on their own terms; instead, they quietly formed their own, smaller firms. The internal challenge Frost faced, in view of these events, was a formidable one: to keep up with the times and the reality that law had become big business—with all of the good and the bad that came with this—required aggressive growth and new practices. But the firm also needed to maintain a connection to the traditions and culture of its past. To balance these interests was not easy by the late 1980s, and it is no surprise that some lawyers believed that the firm's greater capacity to compete in the national and international market had cost it too much in terms of culture.

In May of 1987, this tension prompted eighteen lawyers from the firm's Newport Beach office to depart en masse, saying they wanted a slower pace than the pace that the firm had adopted to maintain its position as the largest Los Angeles corporate law firm and the prestige of being one of the five richest firms in 1986. But for other lawyers, the success was stunning and encouraging. The firm had reached over $156 million in gross revenues and $410,000 in average partner profits. Thereafter, the numbers only continued to mount. By 2008, the firm had grown to 1,000 lawyers, with nearly a billion dollars in gross revenues and fifteen offices around the world.

The groundwork for this subsequent growth and prosperity was laid in the era when the principal architect of the firm's management strategy was F. Daniel Frost. As one colleague noted, "Sometimes I think he just *willed* things to happen."[10] And, as current managing partner Ken Doran has noted, Frost's "vision is still credited [with] taking Gibson, Dunn & Crutcher out of Southern California and . . . on the national stage"; "he left a lasting legacy . . . one that will never be forgotten or adequately repaid."

Vision

Knowing *which* risks to take is not just a matter of consulting one's cultural template and doing the numbers; it requires something much harder to articulate, let alone emulate. Vague and overused, "vision" is often invoked to capture the "something more" that distinguishes a gifted leader from a competent manager or faithful steward of an institution. And even a gifted leader needs economic opportunities, the right colleagues, and plain old luck in order to shine.

Interest in this elusive leadership quality and in why some entities succeed where others fail is always high. Books that offer fresh insights into how leaders and institutions best combine to produce exceptional results often crest on best-seller lists. Malcolm Gladwell's wildly popular book *The Tipping Point* illustrates the enduring interest in these aspects of how management or leadership can produce major shifts across multiple disciplines and scenarios.[11] It identifies the common elements of large social changes that can be effected by small but highly effective teams or groups of individuals. In Gladwell's account, such groups often have four prototypical members: a "Maven" (someone who knows the facts/numbers cold), a "Connector" (someone who is socially adept and might be described as a "six degrees of separation" hub), a "Salesman" or "Persuader" (someone who can make the arguments—with passion—on behalf of the group's vision), and a "Charismatic" (a strong leader who possesses innate magnetism that inspires trust and a desire in others to go wherever he or she is headed).

Applying Gladwell's prototypes to Gibson, Dunn & Crutcher during the 1960s through 1980s suggests that Frost filled the role of the "Charismatic." When he prepared to step down, a reporter for the *Legal Times* who covered the transition noted that "when partners . . . talk about management committee chairman F. Daniel Frost and his contribution to the firm, they almost invariably use the word 'vision.' "[12] But even this account of Frost is too thin. He also had many of the skills and characteristics of the Maven, the Connector, and the Persuader. He knew the numbers (cold); he leveraged his business and social connections (effectively); and he was invested in persuading others of the firm's distinguished past and positive future (passionately). His strong desire to succeed as an individual became infused in the firm. Once he was given the primary leadership role, he drew upon every bit of his abilities and energy to advance the firm, as if his own professional and personal life depended upon its success. And, in a very real way, it did. Frost had become Gibson, Dunn & Crutcher.

This merger between individual and collective identity is often the difference between an ordinary organization and an extraordinary one. Human beings, even in our modern and relatively impersonal age, still gravitate toward places that have distinctive and attractive personalities. But these institutional personalities often depend upon a few especially powerful and dedicated individuals—ones willing to throw their whole selves into the work and the entity. The quality of these individuals in a given organization—how smart and creative they are, how financially astute they are, how wise they are, how fair they are to colleagues, and whether they have integrity—all of this determines what it feels like to work there, and how one measures one's own success within the organization.

Frost had a tremendous investment in the firm's success in every relevant dimension. His western roots and the saddle in the trunk of his car made him care a great deal about whether the firm retained its western character despite the radical changes in California over the years. His family's modest financial means relative to their aspirations made him both prudent and ambitious about assuring that his colleagues were well compensated—extremely so. His "comeuppance" at Andover, as he termed it, made him aware of the ever ascending stratification of academic achievement; he saw what an elite education could provide. But he also had rich and positive experiences in the public sector and even agrarian world. He attended a public law school in Arizona that equipped him fully to succeed among lawyers with the most elite training, and he appreciated that talent is found in a person, not a pedigree. He learned firsthand that the "hungry ones"—people who are not born to a position but who are willing to pursue it vigorously—often will outwork and outperform many others who think a rung on the ladder is their birthright. This often led Frost to favor meritocracy over clubbishness—even as he understood and respected the power of social connections, pursued them, and was willing to use them. Above all, he was a California son, raised in the era of its tremendous, even explosive, growth. He embraced that moment, that energy, that innovative spirit, and that opportunity—and was determined to make an impact there. From this vantage point, he sought to prove something to the East; that the West had something distinctive, something better, to offer the world. It was all of this that led Frost the person to emerge as Frost the "visionary" leader—and the right one—for this firm, at this time.

Transitions

As 1984 dawned, Frost and his colleagues realized he was approaching the date on which the rules would require that he step off of the powerful management committee. Many members became quite anxious about a void in leadership, because they felt no other partner "command[ed] the same degree of respect or wield[ed] the same authority."[13] Others worried that Frost's leadership had been so strong and solitary that no obvious successor had emerged or been groomed to take his post. Still others fretted that Frost would step down formally but continue to rule de facto from behind the curtain. All agreed that it would be difficult to match his achievements as managing partner—itself a deterrent for some would-be heirs. As one Los Angeles lawyer quipped, "Would you want to be the coach to follow John Wooden at UCLA?"

Yet all eras eventually come to an end. Rather than resist or delay his transition from power, Frost surprised his colleagues by precipitating it and stepping down a year before he was obliged to do so, and by steadily relinquishing the reins to others. In this way, he reinforced his promise to turn it over in fact, not just nominally.

In 1986, the firm celebrated Frost's service at a series of events at which they chronicled his years at the firm and the many changes realized during his thirty-five years. When they engaged in the classic "roast" of a senior statesman, nobody laughed harder during the "roasting" segments than Frost himself, who often interjected wry, self-effacing remarks. The programs also included poignant moments as colleagues expressed their appreciation for Frost's able leadership in this profoundly transformative period.

Each of the firm's offices was represented at a formal dinner in Frost's honor, and each presented gifts that reflected their respect for him and his close attention to values and sense of history. One of the notes that accompanied a gift of a series of books on

California history captured this aspect of Frost's leadership and read as follows:

> You brought missionary zeal to your vision of our firm's destiny. You carried the firm's message from Southern California to the national and international scene.
>
> And in the process, you—the pro's pro—became a communicator, a reconciler, as well as a builder.
>
> You gave it your all. And what you built is now and shall be a part of California history.

This eloquent note summarizes the extent of Frost's commitment, and the essence of his legacy: he made history.

As mentioned above, the "young turks" of 1962 knew that regular turnover was healthy and necessary to the firm's ability to adapt to a changing world. They understood, though likely in the dim way that youth anticipate their own maturity and eventual passing, that the new rules they were advocating would one day apply to them as well. Given this awareness, it was entirely consistent with Frost's past practice and stated philosophy for him to step aside as managing partner before reaching the age where this was mandatory. As he prepared for his retirement from the management committee, effective on April 1, 1986, Frost attempted to delegate more of his management responsibilities to other members of the committee, and outlined for the full firm at the 1984 Retreat what he believed would be the major issues that his successor would have to confront.

In addition to accurately predicting the future growth of the firm, and its huge increase in gross revenues, Frost identified in this valedictory address four matters as the most crucial, looming concerns for his successor: first, whether managing lawyers should also be actively engaged in the practice of law; second, whether the firm could continue its no-quota system for new partners; third, whether and how the firm should be reconfigured by the year 2000, in terms of its size, scope of specialties, geographic location, and management structure; and fourth, how the "one firm, one culture" model could be preserved as the firm expanded and practice specialization within the firm continued.

He then offered brief suggestions under each heading—favoring managers who still practice law, recognizing that admission to partner ranks had to be economically sensible, encouraging ongoing analysis of structural issues and willingness to adapt to changed circumstances, and expressing an unequivocal preference for the "one firm, one culture" ethos into the future, regardless of what else might change with time. In other words, he asked the right questions, but was characteristically cautious about answering all but two of them in detail. His two strong answers reflected the reliable guideposts that Frost hewed to throughout his long and successful career.

Frost was a lawyer first and foremost—and an excellent one at that—he believed strongly that future managers should maintain their connection to the practice, in order to lead it wisely and well. One of the most remarkable features of his time as managing partner was that he *did* continue to practice law—indeed, Frost actually led the firm in client billings during his last full year as managing partner, a stunning feat not repeated since, nor likely to be matched ever again in the modern era of law firm managers. Frost's decision to maintain substantial girth in his book of practice, despite his management duties, likely also stemmed from his love of the law. From his first days as a law student, to his years as a library serf, and up until his final days as managing partner, Frost simply loved *being* a lawyer. He saw the role of the lawyer as one of a highly sophisticated problem solver, and he was very, very good at it. He also had inherited a deep respect for the practice of law from the generation of lawyers and professors that mentored him: he did not want to be a bystander to the hands-on work of representing clients.

Frost also took pride in, and derived inspiration from, the firm's

THE ARC OF A LAW FIRM LEADER

history and its shared culture. He emphasized that the firm's western identity—defined dynamically—should never be abandoned. To set that compass by, he believed, would risk losing the firm's distinctiveness, its character, and its human face.

This human face mattered much to Frost, who had made the firm his life—his "family"—for most of adulthood. He defined a leader as someone who could "portray a sense of vision so that everybody is pulling in the same direction," who "gives a common purpose and provides the continuity of the culture, folklore, and heritage." Were Gibson Dunn to lose track of this insight about a common purpose and history, he believed, it would lose track of itself. Thus, although Frost himself believed that "profitability" was the most crucial element of the firm's success, and acted on this belief consistently, his personal fidelity to the firm and sense of the real wellspring of its success derived from the "culture" component.

Moreover, Frost realized that "profitability" can be matched far more easily by a competitor firm than can a firm's character, or its lawyers' sense of a whole larger than themselves. In this way, the ever-present paradox in Frost's personal self again was reflected in his professional planning. To protect the firm he loved and the culture to which he had been drawn himself, he adopted hard-nosed strategies that threatened to undermine that culture's most attractive feature: its sense of community. Yet had he allowed the latter to trump all else, the firm would have foundered in the 1980s. And without the steady growth outward, the firm may not have survived at all, or may have been reduced to a form and scope of influence that Frost would not have considered compelling enough to have devoted thirty-five years of his life to sustaining. This dilemma may explain why many of Frost's colleagues saw him as a complex, Janus-faced figure—alternating between cool detachment and warm, even paternal, gestures that exposed his deep respect and affection for his colleagues.

✦ ✦ ✦

Did Frost achieve a proper balance between these competing impulses? It is now almost a quarter century since Frost's last annual address to the firm, and almost sixty years after he joined the firm. The Gibson, Dunn & Crutcher of today remains both profitable and global. It is still—almost uniquely—carrying no debt. Its current managing partner imparts the long-held cultural standard: "The primary driver of what we do is quality. Quality produces profitability; we don't do the latter first." But its profitability is stunning and was maintained even in the Great Recession.

Most notably, the firm still is "western" in Frost's sense. It's sleekly elegant and modern website includes a link to "Our Story" that emphasizes culture. A video of a member of the firm outlines what she perceives as the Gibson, Dunn & Crutcher "difference." She emphasizes the culture of collaboration, trust, and collegiality. She does not mention Frost in her eloquent and heartfelt account, but she echoes him nonetheless. For Frost was a principal steward and coauthor of that culture, beginning in his youth and continuing until his last day at the helm. As Ron Beard has put it: "Frost saw where the profession was going at an early stage and was bold enough to go after it." His vision, his persistence, his faith in the profession and in his firm, continue to inform the firm's identity even today, and even as it adapts—as it always has, and always must—to the mighty currents of change.

CHAPTER SEVEN

✦ ✦ ✦

Beyond the Firm
New Ventures, and a Legacy of Hope

Frost's lifelong friend, Dr. Peter Bing, sums up Frost as follows: "He is simply well disposed toward life." Bing also describes Frost as extraordinarily principled, entrepreneurial, devoted to the development of young people, and a Renaissance person with an enormously broad set of interests. "Frost," says Bing, has an "energy source—part physical and certainly mental—he loves to do right things and to do lots of them." Moreover, Frost is "activist in any situation he is in."

Such characteristics, of course, do not lead a person to "retire" simply because one set of professional duties ends. It is little surprise that Frost's postlawyering life immediately was filled with a constant stream of projects, and the perpetual setting of new goals. The post-firm phase of his life played out in three principal arenas—business ventures, philanthropy, and a continued interest in western history.

Frost's business ventures included food processing, cattle-feeding enterprises, and investing family resources. In each venture,

Frost did more than invest his money; he applied his curiosity and enormous capacity to absorb details of the business and its people. Having served for decades on the boards of six publicly traded corporations, and having managed a law firm that had over $200 million in gross revenues when he retired as an active partner, Frost had a great deal of knowledge—from a wide variety of industries and business personalities—about how to develop and nurture an investment from start-up to dissolution or sale. He understood the importance of a thorough understanding of one's business and hence learned how each business venture worked, down to "the studs," and quickly could speak knowledgeably and comfortably with veterans in the field—from the owners, to the foremen, to the delivery people. In this regard, he not only replayed his "hands-on" management style from his law firm days, but also emulated the "hands-on" business management style of his friend Stan Avery, who likewise never neglected the details or the people of his industry.

Frost not only had a desire to assure, for the sake of his business investment, that things were running smoothly; he also had a natural interest in how things work that ranged over many topics, many endeavors. This intellectual restlessness and penchant for facts enabled him throughout his life to learn from every client, from every business and social contact, from every case or situation. It predated his time at Gibson, Dunn & Crutcher, though surely was honed there, and carried over fully to his time thereafter.

Frost's geographical restlessness, and his having more time to pursue other interests, also led him to finally satisfy his lifelong yearning for the soil. An investment in agricultural and ranching concerns gave Frost the context in which he could—in a sense—return to his roots, and finally ride in the saddle, rather than merely carry one in the trunk of his car. He invested in the water-rich—an aspect not lost on a lifelong Californian—fields of eastern Washington State, where multiple rivers intersect and provide a constant, reliable source of irrigation for produce. He entered into a partnership with Green Giant foods and processed and marketed asparagus, corn, and other vegetables under that label. He purchased an apple-processing plant that was in bankruptcy—SunRidge Foods—in the Yakima Valley, and began to process and dehydrate apples of various varieties. Both ventures went extraordinarily well, and eventually were taken over by larger businesses by 1995.

The sale of the apple dehydration business to TreeTop was for cash, which Frost promptly invested in Microsoft stock. The stock rose like a rocket, and the bulk of Frost's current fortune today comes from this investment and others made during the 1990s in start-ups—many of which are now household names. That is, Frost became a shrewd venture capitalist whose investments yielded tremendous returns.

In 2000, he began still another company—Rickcy Land & Cattle Company—named after his maternal grandfather, Thomas Rickey. Frost had always been drawn to history, teaching himself about the pioneer roots of his ancestors, the history of California, the chronicles of the many episodes of migration and conflict in the American West. He also had become a vivid storyteller; his accounts of people and events placed them in historical context, with lively descriptions of the characters in question, and nuanced accounts of the motivations and personalities of the people of the story. (For example, when Frost described the imposing Norm Sterry, one could almost see him thundering into the firm's library on a Friday afternoon, looking for the "serf" of the moment to take on the weekend assignment.) In the historical narratives of his ancestors, Frost became particularly nostalgic, and showed his poetic side most visibly.

When Frost began plumbing the archives in Nevada to learn more about Rickey—the legendary figure who loomed so large in his mother's memories, and in Frost's own imagination—he not only was seeking the truth about the infamous arrest of Rickey, but to better understand his own life and times. When he discovered that Rickey had once run a ranching concern under the same name, Frost incorporated his own ranching concern under the name Rickey Land & Cattle, and acquired Rickey's brand. His friend and former client Don Haskell, principal owner of Tejon Ranch, sold Frost a partial interest in its cattle-feeding and financing business in Hereford, Texas, lest Frost be "all hat and no cattle." Frost eventually became the principal owner, and became active in the day-to-day business until he finally decided, at age eighty-three, to sell his interest to several Texas cattlemen and the young and talented manager of the Hereford, Texas, operation. As of 2005, Rickey Land & Cattle thus became an investment company, and Frost officially retired from the cattle business.

Frost's travels after his time at the firm resulted in a personal loss, though also a new path. After leaving California to strike out on these adventures, Frost and his wife, Mia, grew apart. Frost was determined to explore other ventures and venues, whereas Mia's lifelong ties to the Los Angeles arts scene and to California more generally made it impossible for her to contemplate a move away. Frost's drive to live his life at full throttle, now in other regions of the West, took him away from Los Angeles more and more. The couple eventually separated, then divorced.

While looking for a location for one of his food-processing businesses in the Pacific Northwest, Frost was actively recruited by numerous state and local entities with suitable industrial sites and amenities. He ultimately selected a site in Washington that was then owned by the Port of Kennewick. As Frost put it, he "re-potted himself" in Washington. Sue Watkins, longtime manager of the Port, worked with Frost on the project, and over time the business relationship grew into a friendship, and eventually into more. In 1992 they were married.

In addition to her long career in the port business, Sue was active in local, state, and national port, transportation, and industrial issues. She also served on numerous boards and commissions. In 1997 she retired from the port and subsequently from all board positions so that she could preserve time for travel and other pursuits with her husband. Like Frost, Sue applied tremendous energy and intellect to all of her endeavors, and together they created a mutually fulfilling life of travel, business, and philanthropic activities. They now move among three sites—Kennewick, Washington; Tucson, Arizona; and Southern California. In each location, the Frosts take an active interest in local politics, business, and the general well-being of the community.

A primary focus of their recent years has been to promote the educational well-being of the next generation, especially those with the fewest opportunities. Their mission is to assist individual students with exceptional promise but whose families lack the educational background or financial means to support their children's highest aspirations. The Frosts' investment in two projects in particular highlight their commitment to this common cause of improving the life chances of young people through support of education.

HAAP

Frost began the first project of this type in the state of Washington in 1989. The underlying impetus for this program, however, traced back to Frost's California days in two respects. An important influence on Frost's philanthropic direction after he left California was Los Angeles' notorious inability to successfully address its racial and ethnic tensions. Frost was a great admirer of Mayor Tom Bradley and supported his efforts to involve the business community in positive efforts to curb gang activity and offer minority Los Angeles youth alternatives to the strong lures of criminal activity and drugs. But the magnitude of the problem was staggering, and Frost believed Bradley's interventions were "too little, too late." He felt the Los

Angeles project was not a success, in the end, and took the experience to heart.

When Frost observed similar problems beginning to emerge in eastern Washington State, as the Hispanic population surged and the Anglo community began to respond with the kind of animosity toward the Hispanic community that sparks ethnic tensions, he feared the worst. Unlike Los Angeles, however, the east Washington State community was not as sprawling, and the ethnic divides were not yet as flammable. Frost decided, for those reasons, that programs that might have failed in Los Angeles had a chance in Washington. He approached two local leaders—Ruben Lemos and Frank Armijo—and together they began the Hispanic Academic Achievement Program (HAAP) with initial funding from Dan and Sue Frost.

The concept of the program is simple, but highly effective. Every Hispanic public school student, from fifth through twelfth grade, who maintains at least a B average that year, is honored at an annual dinner and awards ceremony sponsored by HAAP. The students and their parents are invited to the dinner, and each honoree is called by name to walk across the stage and receive a certificate. The ceremony often is attended by local dignitaries, and a congratulatory speech is delivered to the students by a prominent Washington official or community leader. The recognition before this ever-growing assembly— in recent years 3,000 students received recognition and more than 10,000 people attended the ceremony—instills pride in the students as well as in their parents, many of whom were not fortunate enough to receive even a basic education. It also models academic diligence for the honorees' peers and siblings. Perhaps most importantly, it affords the female honorees and their sisters much-needed reinforcement of their academic goals, which may enable them to withstand the considerable family and cultural pressure not to attend college, or to in other ways pursue more independent lives. The parents of the girls witness in a public setting their academic achievements and see others recognize and praise this achievement. This slowly helps the community to transform its vision of girls' futures—girls might not need to marry at a young age and devote themselves exclusively to family concerns; some might pursue careers and find fulfillment in other endeavors.

The Frosts believe strongly in the need for such programs as a way of encouraging more minority students to continue on to college. Consequently, they initiated a college scholarship component to the ceremony and began to award a $10,000 scholarship to one outstanding "Frost Scholar" each year—the amount of in-state tuition and books at the University of Washington and Washington State University at the time. The amount of the scholarship later grew to $30,000 to meet the escalating costs of tuition and expenses. The initial screening of applicants was done by the HAAP Executive Committee, which sent three to five names to the final selection committee, chaired by Frost. To attract media and business interest in the program, prominent representatives from both industries also were invited to participate in the selection process. This taught members of the Anglo community about the amazingly talented and dedicated Hispanic students in their local public schools—an experience that helped to open eyes and pierce the veil of unreflective prejudices.

The students who received Frost Scholarships excelled—many later became doctors, engineers, and PhDs. All of the recipients were expected to major in the sciences or mathematics, which reflected the Frosts' belief that these subjects are the best preparation for future careers in the modern economy, and also are ones in which talented students can excel even if English is not their first language. In one remarkable case, a Frost Scholar scored a 760 on the mathematics section of the SAT, and was one of only six students in the state of Washington to receive a Regents Scholarship that year. The student's mother told the Frosts that without their support, her daughter could not have afforded college and may not have pursued it. For this young woman, the impact of the program was truly life altering. Moreover, the Frost leadership gift has inspired many others to contribute to HAAP. By 2009—its twentieth anniversary— the HAAP fund had awarded over $2.5 million in scholarships to regional students.

One Frost Scholarship recipient, Yvette Gutierrez-Morfin, enrolled in Brown University in the fall of 2009. In her letter to the Frosts, thanking them for the scholarship, she said: "I truly don't think I've ever had a better moment in my life than standing on the stage with my brother crying on my left and my mother holding on to my arm and squeezing the life out of it . . . . I would like to thank you for helping me reach my dream of receiving an Ivy League education."

Another impetus for Frost's involvement in philanthropy was personal. As we have seen, his friend Stan Avery taught him the importance of doing good "wholesale, not retail." The Hispanic Academic Achievement Program surely fulfilled that principle: the Frosts' twenty-year investment of over $300,000 yielded not only $2.8 million in support, but a living structure that continues to do communitywide good indefinitely, rather than simply support a single, gifted student. But Frost also may have been motivated by the turbulence of the 1960s. In the age of the California "flower children," the business world, perhaps especially the corporate world, often was seen as a negative force. This view was shared by some of Frost's closest contemporaries and family. Frost, of course, was a business lawyer, and his professional success required him to advance the interests of his well-heeled corporate clients. He later sought to prove to others—if only subconsciously— that one might do good from a position of great influence and affluence and in many ways may be more effective in such a role than by dedicating oneself to others in one-on-one interventions, or—in the case of a lawyer—to public interest law or government. Of course, every public-spirited professional faces a similar challenge: how to hone one's skills and achieve professional and financial success, yet also assure that the ends of one's labors match a more idealistic vision. Frost's post-law-firm days have been devoted to assuring a philanthropic legacy as well as a professional one.

Finally, Frost may be inspired by faith. He is a devout Catholic, who believes in the biblical admonition to assist others less fortunate than oneself. All of these factors—conscious and subconscious—contributed to his decision to actively promote and support the educational success of so many young people and causes.

San Xavier Mission School

A second beneficiary of Frost philanthropy was the San Xavier Mission School in the Tohono O'odham Indian Reservation, just south of Tucson, Arizona. The Frosts bought a home in Tucson in 1997, and began spending winters there because of Frost's arthritis. Once again, their impact on the local community was significant.

The San Xavier Mission School is run by Franciscan Sisters, and the mission itself is the one of the oldest missions in the United States. It was founded by a Jesuit, Father Kino, in the 1700s. Known as "the Dove of the Desert," the mission is a staggeringly beautiful, bone-white structure that can be seen for many miles, gleaming against the austere, brown Sonoran desert landscape.

The O'odham children who attend the mission school are from poor, subsistence-level families. The Frosts adopted an entire class at the school, and began supporting them financially and in terms of other needs—from shoes, to eyeglasses, to trips to the doctor. This initial support then led to a successful capital campaign for a new school building. The Frosts made a significant leadership gift to the campaign, in honor of Frost's younger brother Thomas. Thomas

Frost's picture now hangs in the fifth-grade classroom—a cheerful and airy room—and recognizes his life and service in the navy during World War II.

The Frosts also became close friends with "Sister Jackie" Koenig, the principal of the mission school. Frost was deeply impressed by the sister, whom he believed "walked with God" and was a true saintly presence on earth. When Sister Jackie died of cancer in 2005, Dan and Sue lost a dear friend and a close collaborator in their work for the mission children.

The Frosts, Sister Jackie, and Father Goa of the mission together began a scholarship program modeled after HAAP. Sister Jackie recommended to Dan and Sue one promising elementary school student each year, who was likely to meet the entrance requirements of Tucson's Salpointe High School, a private Catholic high school that places nearly all of its graduates in universities, colleges, and community colleges. The Frosts then supported the successful student's full tuition at the private high school for the entire four years. The students were expected to maintain a B average there, and to otherwise work hard and stay committed to their studies.

Although Salpointe Catholic High School is only a dozen or so miles from the reservation, the leap from home to school is vastly greater for O'odham children than most non-O'odhams can possibly appreciate. Not only is reservation life insular and culturally distinctive; it also is extremely unusual for children from "the rez" to leave the tribe at all, let alone thrive in non-Native contexts. The dropout rate for those few who leave home to attend school elsewhere is very high. The children have few role models or encouragement to succeed in life beyond the reservation, and mainstreaming efforts often fail. The Frosts thus are exceedingly proud of, and have grown especially close to Wynona Peters—a Frost Scholar who not only succeeded at Salpointe High, but went on to become a student at the University of San Diego, where she won a McNair scholarship in her junior year and participated in a research project on the impact of alcoholism on the reservation—one of the health crises these tribes currently face.

Peters was a standout at Salpointe High, excelling in athletics as well as academics. She played on the school's varsity basketball team as a freshman, was a star runner on the track team, and was admired and loved by her classmates and faculty. She also was elected by the elders of her tribe at age fourteen to be the princess of the tribe. This is a high honor that carries significant responsibility: to learn the crafts, traditions, and language of the tribe. (Tribal leaders have told Frost that she may one day become the elected tribal chief.) The Frosts view Peters as a miraculous young person who has overcome staggering odds to pursue her goals. Their relationship with Peters is a close and loving one, and the philanthropic investment in her education is a true matter of the heart.

Perhaps the greatest gift to the Frosts, however, apart from the personal pleasure they derive from improving the lives of these young people, has been the tribe's respect. Among Native people, trust is hard to earn, so when the tribe sent the following message to the Frosts in 2007, the couple considered it a high accolade:

> The day you were born God danced and we continue to dance
> for your unselfishness in providing for and supporting our Native
> American children.

Other Gifts, Other Beneficiaries

Though HAAP and the Mission captured Frost's heart, he has not neglected other worthy causes along the way. He has been a significant donor to the UCLA Medical Center, where he receives his primary medical care.

The city of Kennewick, Washington, now boasts a gleaming and much needed 55,500-square-foot municipal building that sits on more than seven acres, thanks to a Frost gift. Frost donated a food-processing plant, which the city remodeled to support municipal offices. A grateful city named the building the "Dan Frost Municipal Services Campus," and Russ Burtner, executive director of municipal services, estimates that the $6 million donation saved the taxpayers as much as $15 million—the estimated cost of pursuing options for the badly needed facility. Forgoing the rent they could have received on the industrial facility, which was constructed in 1989 and in excellent shape, Frost instead gifted the property to a city where the couple spends much of the year, and in which Sue Frost has been a prominent leader for decades. As Burtner put it, "Frost saw the need in a community that he adopted and he stepped up." The gift was all the more striking, said Burtner, because it was not to a typical philanthropy or not-for-profit, but to a municipality. Few people, if any, think of a city's needs in this way, or consider the importance to city employees of the quality of the physical surroundings in which they work, day after day. The Frost gift not only saved the taxpayers money; it also improved the lives of city workers.

At his alma mater, the University of Arizona, Frost likewise has been generous, and often honored for his professional success and manifold contributions. Most notably, he received one of the university's highest honors when he was selected as a recipient of the Centennial Medal—given to the 100 most distinguished graduates in the university's 100-year history.

Frost also was a longtime member, and served as president, of the College of Law's National Board of Visitors. He established a student award in honor of his friend and former dean, S. Thomas Sullivan, and became one of the school's most steadfast supporters. In 2009, Frost initiated still another law school scholarship program, in support of an especially promising first-year student. The first "Frost Scholar" at the College of Law began in the fall of 2009 and is expected to carry on his legacy of academic achievement, professional distinction, community leadership, and philanthropy.

Finally, Frost has offered his counsel to every dean in the college's nearly 100-year history since its first dean, Samuel Fegtly. The college records include correspondence during World War II between Frost and Dean J. Byron McCormick—who later became president of the University of Arizona. These letters convey young Frost's sense of duty, his desire to share with his professors his professional progress, and also his hope that students who came after him might strike out beyond Arizona and be similarly successful. As a young lawyer, he offered to head up alumni gatherings in California to enable graduates to network there, and suggested how the college might better place Arizona law graduates in the California market. He later recommended curricular changes for students interested in business law and did what he could to serve the college and to expand its growing national and international influence.

At every turn, and in multiple ways, Frost thus invested his prodigious energy in cutting a wider path for others—to "level the playing field," as he put it. He recognized how competitive the business world can be and how difficult it is for people who are not born into great wealth or tutored in elite educational settings to advance to the highest and most influential levels of professional leadership. Frost pulled—sometimes pushed—others along. To again quote Dr. Bing, he "liked to do good things and *a lot of* good things."

As usual, Frost was not a "passive investor" in these endeavors: he watched carefully over his projects and its people, just as he did over the firm and its lawyers. He advised, encouraged, turned seed money into self-sustaining endowments, expressed concern when he believed decisions were unwise, and in every instance was an important advisor to the entities and individuals he supported.

✦ ✦ ✦

Now in his late eighties, Frost still is engaged in similar pursuits and still is physically imposing and mentally vigorous. He has the energy of a person half his age, despite significant back issues from arthritis. He arrives early for every meeting exceedingly well prepared for the discussion, with a long list of questions, points to cover, and concerns on a neatly folded piece of paper that he withdraws from his breast pocket. His curly gray hair often is matted down from his well-worn, brown cowboy hat. One still can see in Frost the managing partner of his Los Angeles office, handling the firm's matters with his quick intellect, easy command of the relevant facts, and uncanny ability to foresee how present actions may produce future consequences. He offers advice—unvarnished and straightforward—to help others make business decisions and engage in successful planning efforts. Few, if any, of the not-for-profits to which he donates his time could afford to hire him to obtain the same good counsel; none of them can afford not to heed it. In short, he is ever the "managing partner," who still worries if he is not worried, and seeks to help less experienced, nonprofessional managers see the obstacles ahead and how to navigate them in order to achieve their higher goals.

On a personal level, Frost continues to thrive. His life with his wife, Sue—enjoyed without the massive demands of being managing partner of a global law firm—is a fulfilling one that is still evolving.

Of course a long life also includes personal losses. These, too, have shaped Frost.

Most recently, Frost was profoundly affected by the death of his son, Daniel Blackburn Frost. His son was a much admired surgical oncologist in California who contracted Parkinson's disease at an early age and suffered for twenty years from the debilitating disease.

In July of 2009, at the young age of sixty, Frost's son succumbed to the disease. Frost wrote Dr. Frost's obituary, which read, in part, as follows:

Dr. Frost is the great-great grandson of Daniel Blackburn, one of the founders of Paso Robles, California. His great-great granduncle was William Blackburn, a lieutenant with General Freemont in the Bear Flag Revolution, and later the first Alcalde of Santa Cruz in the new State of California. He is also a great grandson of Thomas B. Rickey, a pioneer Nevada cattleman, legislator and banker.

Dr. Frost was born in Los Angeles, California on May 29, 1949. He grew up in Altadena, California. He graduated from Polytechnic School in Pasadena, California, where he won honors in physics and mathematics. He also won numerous varsity letters in soccer and track. He then attended Williams College, Williamstown, Massachusetts, graduating with honors in pre-medical studies. He received his medical degree from the School of Medicine at the University of California at Los Angeles and took his residency at Los Angeles County Hospital.

Subsequent to his general residency, Dr. Frost fulfilled his military requirement by serving in the United States Public Health Service as a general practitioner in residence on the Navajo Reservation in Window Rock, Arizona. After serving there for a year, he was transferred as a Lieutenant Commander in the U.S. Naval Reserve to the Long Beach Naval Hospital, where he completed his tour of duty.

By that time, Dr. Frost had decided he wanted to become a surgical oncologist and, therefore, served a number of fellowships in that discipline culminating in a fellowship at the famous cancer center, MD Anderson Hospital in Houston, Texas. For his work during that fellowship, he won an award from The Society of Surgical Oncologists for his original research in surgical oncology. He then became a staff surgical oncologist with the Kaiser Medical Group where he practiced until his Parkinson's disease prevented him from doing so. During this period, Dr. Frost wrote and lectured widely in surgical oncology in the United States, the U.K. and Europe. He authored and co-authored many medical papers as well as chapters for medical textbooks.

Frost very much wanted his son to be remembered for his many virtues. One also can see in this eloquent tribute Frost's own values—respect for family heritage, for professional accomplishments, and for fulfillment of duties to country and to society more generally.

Dr. Frost requested that his ashes be scattered at sea, and that John Lennon's "Let It Be" be played at his funeral service.[1] True to his wishes, the memorial service ended with a performance of Lennon's famous ballad. His father delivered the eulogy, which closed with the following lines:

> When word of Dan's death spread through his circle of friends, colleagues and family, they cried the rain down that night. He will be remembered forever for his character, his honor, his humor, his fortitude, his kindness, his surgical skills, the many lives he saved, and his research that brought hope and help to so many.

The family later fulfilled Dr. Frost's wish for a burial at sea.[2]

✦ ✦ ✦

CHAPTER EIGHT

Final Reflections, Enduring Lessons

S ince leaving full-time practice in 1988, Frost has remained in
touch with his successors at Gibson, Dunn & Crutcher. The
current managing partner, Ken Doran, has become a friend,
and someone for whom Frost has tremendous respect. Few people
likely understand better than Frost does what pressures Doran faces,
as the world suffered what has been dubbed the Great Recession—
(capitalization marking the gravity of the period and its profound
challenges). The California economy sank precipitously in 2008, and
the aftermath of this recession endures. Whether this was a temporary setback, or a degradation that will dim the prospects for future
lawyers and other professionals indefinitely, remains unclear.

Of course, law firms prosper only when their clients prosper.
If American industries fail to fully recover, then the law firms that
today are furloughing colleagues, delaying associate start dates, and
laying off attorneys also will not fully recover. At the same time,
the cost of higher education continues to spiral upward, outpacing
inflation. In the difficult years ahead, it thus will be much harder for

bright students to afford college, let alone legal education. This will mean fewer law school graduates from middle-class or lower-class families, and higher student loan debt for nearly all who do graduate. Many of these graduates will be seeking private law firm jobs, as they always have. But more of them than ever before will *need* such jobs, in order to pay off their education debts. Even the elite private law firms today still are feeling the pressures of the recent recession, and few are able to promise the kind of "profitability" that Frost created for his lawyers during his reign as the firm's leader.[1]

Gibson Dunn must navigate through these choppy waters and must determine the optimal balance between culture and adaptation, between profitability and austerity, between optimism and healthy skepticism about the economic future. It must maintain morale, despite the grim economic headlines, and adjust its vision as new circumstances warrant.

As it does, and as Doran and his successors determine how to best steer the firm, and consider what their own biographies as a leaders might include, they might consider the guideposts from Frost's life and work.

In short form, the Frost leadership elements were as follows. He demonstrated a combination of (1) vision; (2) respect for the context, history, and culture of the firm; (3) ability to state a strategic plan simply, widely, consistently; (4) a commitment to profitability; (5) commitment to quality service and devotion to client needs; (6) consistent diversification of risk; (7) awareness that the economy cycles; and (8) passion.

Frost knew that a leader must look backward and forward at once, and remove the blinders of the present when tacking. A respect for nature's forces, and for the rise and fall of business, is the first step to riding these waves, and harnessing the forces rather than being overcome by them.

Frost also recognized an abiding human need for connection.

In every human enterprise—despite technological innovations that render organizations more teleological, more virtual, and less corporeal—people still need a sense of belonging and common enterprise in order to do their best work. One of the most complicated tasks for modern leaders is to capture this enduring, even primitive human need and apply it to a rapidly changing, often virtual, globalized culture. Frost understood this need for connection and wedded his business vision with an almost mythical notion of the firm, of the West, of his roots. That is, Frost maintained throughout his career an *idea* of Gibson, Dunn & Crutcher—more aspirational, perhaps, than fully attainable. Such aspirational concepts propel people forward in every endeavor, in any historical moment. The task of articulating these aspirations is quintessentially a leader's responsibility.

By themselves, of course, aspirational statements will not suffice to lift a firm, a fund, or a family to a higher plane. One also needs resources, able colleagues, and a sound strategy. But without a leader who can articulate an aspirational goal that calls to mind a higher plane or purpose, even the best team is unlikely to truly excel or, even in some cases, survive.

Finally, Frost seized the day. In every relation and in every context, he used the opportunity to learn, to create social capital, and to leverage his connections for business development ends.

Even in his later years, Frost still invests in others and becomes involved in multiple communities and concerns. He lives fully and greets each new challenge energetically. The ultimate key to his endurance and his success is not merely good genes or good fortune, but a habit of facing *outward* and *forward*.

Modern law firm leaders must observe all of these principles. They too must continue to offer a service that the world needs and take excellent care of their clients' interests. They too must know their own business and the numbers—cold—while also being able to command the respect and loyalty of their colleagues. As leaders, they must be able to articulate their mission convincingly and succinctly.

They also need to give their colleagues a sense of involvement. All firm members—lawyers and nonlawyers—must know where the firm is going, how progress will be measured, and whether goals have been achieved. This is even more true in today's weak economy than in yesterday's robust one, because firms today have less ability to inspire performance by the vastly simpler morale-boosting method of steadily increasing compensation. Today, the attractions will be to the energy, the quality of the work and one's colleagues, and the *relative* profitability and quality of life that a firm can offer. These substitutes for income escalation are much harder to produce and will require more imagination and greater commitments of the firm leaders' time and energy—to assure that all members of "the team" feel the firm's interest, support, and respect, and are dedicated to its goals.

If Frost were still at the helm in this changed environment, what would he do to maintain his own firm's momentum? Most likely, he would adhere to the core principles that enabled him to negotiate the shoals decades ago. Modern leaders would do well to hew to them as well.

APPENDIXES

✦ ✦ ✦

✦ ✦ ✦

Family Tree of F. Daniel Frost

FAMILY TREE OF F. DANIEL FROST

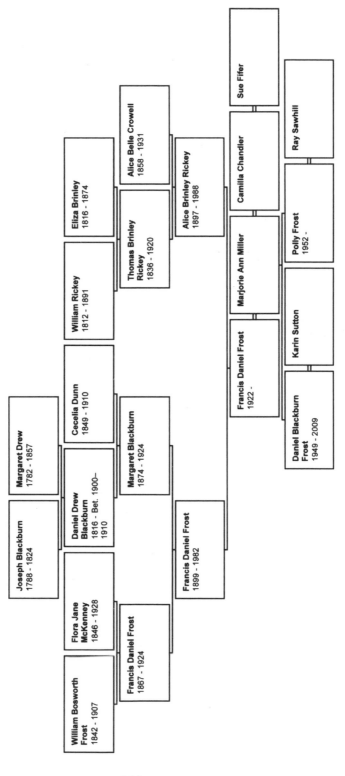

✦ ✦ ✦

The Arc of Law Firm Leadership

Appendix B1. 1980 Retreat Speech by F. Daniel Frost

Introduction

The role of the prophet in human affairs is never a very happy one. The odds are surely against him.

Unexpected developments and new trends and approaches are bound to overtake him.

But there is a difference between prophecy and planning. We cannot hide behind the uncertainties of the future.

We must look ahead and we must plan, and always be aware that we must change our plans in the light of unfolding events.

Of one thing we can be certain—the firms that will do the best during the '80s—in fact the firms that will survive the '80s in the heat of competition and changes—are right now trying to work out their strategy, including strategizing about how to dominate the legal profession in Southern California.

Having said that much, I feel I must also add that it has been a very sobering experience for me to go from the expansion mode talks and vote we had in Los Angeles in early September—to go from that heady experience to two weeks on the continent as counsel for a couple of international companies. There is heavy concern in the UK—and in Europe about the possibility of no growth of the economy *generally* during all of the '80s. They have great concern and caution about the U.S. economy.

This has been a good reminder to me that we must still plan for cyclical growth—not to expand too fast as well as not too slow—hard judgments that we have not always called perfectly in the past—but we have done fairly well.

The legal profession is often called the last of the cottage industries—or the profession of the quill pen.

But the 1980s will, unfortunately in a way, put an end to this romantic notion of the practice of law.

I would like to talk today about some of these changes, how they affect GD&C, and the future we are trying to plan for the 1980s.

But first let us look at the condition of the legal profession.

Some recent writers have indicated that the condition of the bar in California is chaotic. For example, according to my friend Marianne Pfaelzer, a good friend of the governor, this chaos has been brought on intentionally by the governor, who she feels is hostile to the bar, particularly the large firms. (For example the proposal to disallow the use of nonpracticing or deceased partners names in the name of the law firm.)

As you know, we have seen huge increases in the bar—virtually a doubling in the last five years. A very high proportion compared to New York. Further, it has been observed that we have a two-, three- or four-tiered bar—the haves and the have-nots—a dangerous situation, perhaps modified by legislation for prepaid legal plans, a great increase in legal aid, etc. And we could become very unpopular as a large international law firm which could have political repercussions.

Next we must look to the competition from our peers. We have already talked about the incursion into Southern California by out-of-state firms. Enough to say, this will continue.

Corporate legal departments are having tremendous growth, and this will continue. Perhaps into specialties as well as litigation.

Perhaps a slowdown in the current proliferation of new legislation.

Perhaps the curtailment of lengthy discovery by federal judges.

Changes in trying PI cases.

But no abatement in the complexity of our society and world, nor in the size of business organizations or the importance of international expertise and the representation of foreign governments and citizens.

There has been no abatement of the importance of the international money markets.

There has been no abatement in the tremendous advances in technology.

And there has been no abatement in the significance of the Pacific Rim, Middle East, and other parts of the world.

If I am right in this analysis—it tells me we must do the following during the '80s.

A. Become more involved in state and bar politics to protect ourselves to the extent possible.

B. Expand our office coverage in California so we can offer total California services—the biggest state—richest state and state of the future. This means at least a Sacramento office.

C. Should expect some decrease in rate of growth of litigation department—to be made up by international and specialties, i.e., entertainment, employee benefits, special corporate work, etc. We should expand our sophistication in government affairs and other specialized abilities—FCC, Department of Energy and similar administrative work, oil and gas—Denver? Texas, Atlanta, Far East.

D. Expand selling of total services.

E. Expand representation of smaller, emerging companies, especially in high technology—San Jose, San Diego.

F. Expand our foreign capabilities.

Why do these things?

A. Firm healthy from financial viewpoint.

B. Would give opportunities to associates and younger partners to handle quality work.

C. Economy of size to control cost of legal services and be able to afford new equipment—quality backup.

D. Be at forefront of new concepts, i.e., evolutionary management systems.

E. Be able to offer total legal services to clients nationwide.

I think it would be a disastrous course of action for this firm to spend its time fighting rearguard actions versus these changes, i.e., corporate law departments or new technology.

I think we know better than most—perhaps best of all—how to achieve a synergistic effect from the combination of specialties, multi-offices, and a traditional law practice.

In this regard, profitability is a good discipline for efficiency—if highly profitable *and* good client relations—this means we're doing it right.

We have followed for the past two to three years a deliberate policy to position ourselves for the '80s.

A successful firm has to grow.

By definition—means new clients

Increase in number of partners—tenure—giving opportunity for associates.

Multioffices make this possible—on office alone couldn't do it.

Seven percent increase in shares including raises and new partners.

To afford this plus inflation, need growth of revenues and net.

Some resent growth—but if we think through, this means opportunity for the young.

Goal for 1990—recognized as one of half dozen most competent, most prestigious, most influential, most powerful and most profitable law firms in the U.S.

And yet preserve our character.

Who we are. Obviously opinions can differ but I would like to give you my description of who we are and what distinguishes us from our colleague law firms.

First of all, we are an old western firm—ninety years of existence is nothing by eastern, midwestern or, of course, European standards—but it is very old for Los Angeles.

Being western in character, we are informal, we believe in informality in our dealings with each other—collegial—friendly—first-name basis.

Being an old firm we have many ties to the past that bind the partnership together.

We are hardworking.

We are dedicated to serving our clients.

In our personal lives, almost without exception, we are attuned to the out of doors—a love of the land and the sea is a common interest.

We have never hired anyone for their social connections—although our colleagues think of us as being deeply involved in the community— and we are—but this came about through effort and leadership.

We are not geared to one political party.

We are careful—we are productive and we are very aggressive but in a quiet way.

We are very sophisticated in the law.

But our basic characteristic is still summed up when one says we are an old western firm—regardless of where our people are—that is our personality.

Who we are

A steadily growing old western law firm providing high-quality, sophisticated legal services on a national and international basis.

Old in years—young in nature

What does all this mean?

1. Old is relative

Tradition—pride

2. Western—informal—not stratified—partners and associates participating in decisions—i.e., retreats

3. Young in nature—aggressive, opportunistic, hardworking

4. Growing—opportunities for young lawyers—important to grow but not too fast

5. Mobility—don't have to wait for a death to advance

6. National and international

The challenge is to preserve our heredity—our character—and yet to meet the challenges of the '80s.

Where we are

I don't want to brag about what a good job we are doing—nobody dislikes those kinds of speeches more than I do—but I think we should take a few minutes to look at some of the good things that our firm has accomplished in the last ten or so years.

A. We have kept up a steady rate of growth to meet our needs—resulting in an increase in lawyers in virtually every year including the year 1979 to 1980, when many firms had negative growth or no growth.

B. It appears this trend will continue in the near future despite poor economic conditions in the US, UK, and Europe.

C. Unlike other firms, our partner distributions have grown in real income in the past decade—our income per share has stayed ahead of inflation in actual dollars despite the worst inflation in the history of our country. Income per share has risen from $1,223 in 1969 to $2,406 in 1979.

D. We have increased the quality of our workload to the highest level in its history.

E. We have financed an enormous growth in capital improvements with absolutely first-class branch offices—and we have done it with internal cash flow; our only borrowing is an investment in Crocker Center. This is an enormous achievement, I think unequaled by any other firm.

F. Our offices are of equal quality to any offices of any law firm.

G. We have the finest administrative staff.

H. We are positioned to meet the growth in international business.

I. All of our offices contribute to the profits of the firm.

J. We are on the road to funding our retirement and death benefit program.

On the negative side, I would list the following—by no means unique to our firm.

A. Many lawyers in the firm still resist the concept that we are a business as well as a profession. But we must make money in order to stay in existence—and that means selecting clients who can and will pay our fees, keeping current time records, making timely billings, etc. I remember the days in the firm when some of the very senior partners would go through the overhead if we asked them to keep time records or we mentioned that we are a business as well as a profession. I think the new generation of partners has little trouble in seeing this. However, I know that many partners hate the billing process—but it is not difficult once we learn the discipline. And again, I am interested to note it is the older lawyers who are the worst offenders.

B. We probably have a partnership ratio we cannot maintain.

C. Our workload for middle partners is too high.

D. Our style of governance probably needs to be revised to be sure that it is as participatory as possible—and yet still viable on a day-to-day basis without wasting lawyers' time.

E. Out younger lawyers must position themselves in the profession and in the community when the current leadership has retired.

Other Problems

1. Tremendous growth in attorneys in California—haves and have-nots

2. Corporate legal departments

A. Better

B. Broader

C. Want to use their own people

D. Huge pressures to reduce costs of outside counsel

3. Decrease in discovery

4. Increase in arbitration as in other countries

5. Slowdown in new laws

6. Competition in LA for our traditional high-quality business—brazen solicitation by other firms.

7. Profitability pressures—higher costs of associates and lay staff, causing a drag on our margins.

Where we are going

A. *Why Expand?*

1. Changes in legal practice—fewer referrals from out-of-state firms—increase in out-of-state firms in Los Angeles—importance of providing clients legal services in New York and Washington

2. Concept of specialization requiring different geographic locations

3. Protect from business cycles—financial strength to afford best

4. Opportunity for young lawyers

5. Economy of size to counteract exploding costs

6. Being able to increase income per share—the glue that holds the firm together (in this regard I predict the disappearance of some firms because of bad financial management)

7. Avoid conflicts without stifling us

Conclusion

1. Cannot fight growth—wouldn't want to

2. But can control

3. Disastrous to fight rearguard action against changes in the practice

4. We must be fast on our feet to predict and adjust to these changes

5. We know better than most how to get synergistic effect from branches and specialties

So the picture I see in 1990 is a firm of at least 400—probably 500 lawyers—a few more U.S. offices—a few more small foreign offices—a great increase in specialization—and on our 100th anniversary in 1990 we will have achieved the goals I have described.

Appendix B2. 1981 Retreat Speech by F. Daniel Frost

My fellow partners—greetings.

I would like to start out by saying that I think the principal topic of discussion for this retreat—firm governance—is an excellent and timely subject. Although probably for as long as the firm has had a written partnership agreement ultimate authority has vested in the executive committee—nevertheless within such traditional limitation the *procedure* of governance—the *style* of governance—has continually evolved, and it is important that this evolution continue.

This year the revenues of the firm will total about $53 million. By 1987—assuming we can continue our momentum—we should be grossing about $100 million. Traditionally that will mean a net income of from $40 to $50 million. It means our overhead will be running about $4 to $5 million a month. That makes the firm a very major business by any yardstick.

I think those figures give us all a sense of the absolute need to have the business side of the governance of the firm in the hands of highly qualified, business-oriented people, by that I mean people who are cost minded and profit oriented.

There is and will be an *equal* need to have the professional side of the governance of the firm—the recruiting, supervision, and training of lawyers—managed by lawyers who are highly skilled in these areas.

In addition, there must be a group to receive input from the business and professional sides to decide professional compensation matters on an actual—and perceived to be—fair and equitable basis.

Next, there is a need to have some person or small group intensely interested in and skillful in strategic planning, including the coordination of client development.

And lastly, there must be a person or small group to coordinate all of these activities in an orderly fashion and to pull all aspects and branches of the firm together into a smooth running whole. This is the leadership side of governance.

Obviously, one or more of these activities can be placed in the same person or group, but not all of them.

It seems to me that we have, and will always have, partners of this firm who can perform these functions. I refuse to believe that a non-lawyer chief executive officer is the only long-term answer for governance—at least for this law firm.

To function properly all of these activities need the best staff possible. I am proud to say that we have such a staff. As time goes on, the organization of staff will really depend on the operating style of those in governance. For us, the troika style has worked very well.

Obviously, the best lawyers, or the most senior lawyers, are not necessarily the best at governance. Further, those who are the best teachers or recruiters might well not be the best businessmen and vice versa.

The problem is how to identify the best talent for these different aspects of governance. That in my view is the ultimate key question. And this selection must always take into account the dynamics of the firm—the interaction of the partners to each other and to those in governance.

I am sure that these problems will receive a good airing at this retreat.

I might make a few observations on what the job of governance requires in the sense of leadership. First of all, I think it is important for those in all areas of governance to also be practicing law. As the firm gets larger, I recognize that this might not be possible, except on a reduced basis. Nevertheless, I believe it is worth the effort because the ties to client's problems and thinking give the lawyer a much better feel for the needs of clients and of the firm and of what the practice of law is currently all about. Certainly continuing to practice law gives those in governance a better rapport with the other lawyers in the firm and a better chance to evaluate them, and to understand them and their needs and problems. If I am right about this, then the job of governance will always be a very high-energy job, and one of long hours. No one can do all that should be done.

The job possibly could be filled on a less time-consuming and high-energy basis, but in my opinion it would be to the detriment of the firm. I am only mentioning these factors to make the point that I feel the current five-year term for the management committee is correct. The baton needs to be passed to fresh runners. Otherwise the firm will falter, reflecting the fatigue or staleness of those in governance. . . . That is why at the 1984 retreat I expect you will see an entirely different group of people on the management committee.

Earlier I mentioned that the procedure and style of governance have evolved. This evolution has turned to a great extent on the desires and personalities of those on the executive committee who have been most interested in governance. I think it is fair to say that the history of the governance of this firm can really be divided into three phases. The period: 1890 to 1936. The HFS period: 1936 to 1968, and the post-HFS period: from 1968 to the present.

During the first forty-six years of the firm the partnership consisted of a group of individuals loosely practicing law together—some of whom were giants in the history of the Bar of Southern California. Jim Gibson, Billy Dunn, Albert Crutcher, Sam Haskins, Norman Sterry, Elmo Conley, Henry Prince, and others. From listening to Herbert Sturdy I gather that during this period there was very little firm organization, no time sheets, billings when and if the partner felt like it, little overhead cost, and virtually no associate compensation. This might be called the golden period by some.

When Herbert became a partner in the early or midthirties he quickly took a role in governance—by interest and by force of intellect and personality. He even induced Sam Haskins and Norman Sterry to keep time records. He started simple business controls. He and his colleagues—Homer Crotty, Stuart Neary, Jack McFarland and others, plus the old guard—moved the firm forward through and just after World War II.

This was certainly a period of extreme centralization and control. It was a holding period and not a growth period. Herbert made the compensation decisions for years. He did the recruiting for years; the firm became more formal and institutionalized with three classes of partners, including the concept that the senior partners administered the firm.

In the late '50s and early '60s Herbert responded to the youth movement of the time and gradually led the firm away from one-man control and into a period of growth. A retirement program was gradually instituted. The concept was established that committees of the firm shall be given considerable authority. It was then that the compensation committee, the law school committee, the financial management committee and other committees came into their own. Herbert was one of the first to recognize the need for professional staff and brought to the firm Herb Schwab, who added a very constructive influence to the administration of the firm. It was during this period that the first branches were instituted.

During the post-HFS period the committees have rapidly multiplied and there has been a gradual trend towards strong participation in the administration of the firm from outside the executive committee. The professional development committee—the law school committee—the branch partners committee—the retreat committee—all exert an enormous influence on the firm. The firm today could not exist without the work product of these committees. And I am very pleased to note that next week the management committee and the newly formed and elected advisory committee will have their first joint meeting. We expect a great deal from this committee.

I would characterize the executive committee today as being close to the model of a board of directors—receiving information and recommendations from various committees, then making decisions. The conclusion was reached over three years ago that this committee was too large to self-manage the firm. The leadership responsibility must be somewhere else. This gave rise to the management committee. . . .

Let's now turn to the future of the firm as to the practice of law. I would like to briefly sketch our overall plan for the ten-year period 1975 to 1985 and answer some common questions that arise in connection with this plan.

When I use the word "plan" in this context, I mean it in the sense of a road map showing where we came from and where we want to be in 1985. Specific details as to the journey have to await conditions as they arise. And this type of plan should be distinguished from a financial forecast or budget, short-term recruiting goals, or the estimates we make for space planning and staff probabilities in all of our offices. Those matters are details and predictions that help us plot our course but do not tell us where we want to be.

The overall plan or goal of the firm is two pronged—to have a firm that has the ability, and is recognized as having the ability, to deliver legal services of the highest quality in the major industrial and financial areas of the world. Secondly, to have recognized ability as being highly skilled in the most important, sophisticated, and specialized areas of the law.

In achieving this two-prong goal, we seek to have an international reputation for the quality of our professional services, of our clients and legal assignments, of the opportunity for professional growth and achievement for younger lawyers and the quality of the environment for the practice of law. We are not trying to be the biggest law firm— we *are* trying to be the best law firm. Excellence is our goal. We see ourselves as marching to our own drummer, not following any other firm's pattern, not being slavish to the latest trends, not competing with any other particular firm—but rather going our own way. We intend to be opportunistic, we intend to be on the cutting edge of the law and the technology that supports the practice of law. We intend to continue being one of the most profitable law firms in the United States. We intend to continue the stability of the share—with the goal of continuing to have it at least keep pace with the rate of inflation. We feel profitability and share stability are high-priority items not only because they are important factors in themselves in holding this great firm together, but also because they provide a discipline for efficiency.

We started with an old high-quality regional firm that had many of the traditional skills but was far from able to cover all important areas of the law. So we had geographic and skills goals to achieve.

By 1985 we hope to have the framework necessary as to the delivery of legal services; it will include most, if not all, of the United States, UK, Europe, the Middle East, and the Far East. It will probably not include New York or any additional branches in the U.S. And definitely will not include South America, Mexico, Africa, and many other legal markets that in the future our people in governance will want to take a look at.

In the area of specialties, we have greatly broadened the scope of the firm. But again, there will be much to do in the future. For example, the field of communications law is an area that we should be in by 1985 but might well not be.

But by 1985 the nucleus should be formed for a great national and international firm that does have the ability to practice a very broad scope of specialties. Also by 1985 we hope to have back in the firm the partners and associates now with the government. They will bring to the firm an added perspective and expertise that will be very useful to us.

It is important that these goals be achieved within the framework of our traditional values and without weakening the financial structure of the firm.

We recognize that that is a lot to try to achieve in a ten-year span. We are more than halfway there in time and have almost all of this framework now in place. Therefore the next few years should be primarily devoted to *consolidation.*

Before going on I would like to point out that our overall plan is not based upon achieving a specified growth rate. I see no point in saying we want to have 400 lawyers at a certain date and 500 lawyers at a certain later date. The actual size of a law firm by itself doesn't mean anything. On the other hand, if we can achieve the goals I have outlined, then the growth of the firm—the health and future of the firm—will take care of themselves.

Now everything that I have said is subject to the constraint that we want to achieve these results within the existing policies of the firm. We want to preserve the character of the firm. Although we have achieved enormous strength and success and pleasure through the lateral associations into the partnerships that have been made in recent years, we intend to severely restrict such situations to individual lawyers and only where we cannot fill a particular need from within the firm. I believe there is a broad consensus within the firm against the merger with another firm, whatever the need and whatever the size of the other firm.

I believe that over the next five to ten years this may cause us to lose our standing vis-à-vis other firms as to size, but so be it. I do expect a wave of mergers to appear. In fact, this trend is already starting.

I talked at the last retreat as to why we felt the move to a national and international firm was important. I believe that debate is over and a broad consensus of the firm supports what has occurred. It should be kept in mind that our strategy in this regard is not to create a series of regional offices, but rather to have branches, outside of our home base, each of which contributes something to the whole and not to just repeat in each branch what occurs in the other. Our home base we define as Southern California, being Los Angeles, Century City, Newport Center, and San Diego. The contributions of the branches to the whole were planned as follows:

Washington, D.C.	To headquarter our international law practice as well as having a broad practice of the law on the East Coast.
San Jose	To headquarter our practice vis-à-vis high technology companies and venture capital companies as well as to conduct a broad practice of the law in Northern California.
Denver	To headquarter our natural resources practice which we will conduct on a national basis—and again to have a broad practice in the Rocky Mountains area. In this connection it is interesting to note that more and more one reads in the literature that Denver has become the center of energy for the United States, surpassing both Houston and Dallas. Our serious planning for Denver began about the time of last year's retreat mentioned in my comments. Enormous effort has gone into this major step. The more we see and learn about Denver, the more convinced we are that this is a most significant chapter in the firm's history. I know that George, Charlie, and Lee agree.

London	To allow the firm as a whole to benefit from ties to that world financial center.
Paris	To allow the firm as a whole to benefit from ties to Europe and the Common Market.
Riyadh	To allow the firm as a whole to benefit from ties to the Middle East.

By 1984 we hope to be able to tie the firm to the Far East in the same manner.

Combined with this strategy as to branching is our concept of seeking out areas of opportunity in specialized areas of practice. Recently we not only established our natural resources group, but also a financial institutions group and a group to handle business from the Far East on both an onshore and offshore basis.

We have spoken in the past of how the synergistic effect of these moves has had an absolutely outstanding effect on the business of the firm and on the quality of the practice of the firm as a whole.

We believe that each of these steps has increased the reputation of the firm, the quality of our practice, and the opportunities for advancement throughout the firm. Our progress is carefully monitored. Every three months we have a three- or four-hour meeting of the branch partners in charge to review results versus budgets and to provide a round table discussion of what is going on. The branch partners in charge then call a meeting of the other partners in the particular branch and relay that information to them. In my view these meetings have been outstanding in every way.

Now turning to the questions frequently raised that I mentioned. These seem to be the following:

Question: Why are we seeking out new areas of opportunity when we are already so busy?

Question: As a corollary shouldn't we stop seeking new business and consolidate what we have?

Question: If the undertaking of a new opportunity means the lateral entry of a partner or associate, should we undertake it?

Question: Are we moving so fast that we are losing the traditional identity of Gibson, Dunn & Crutcher?

Question: Does our overall strategy put us into a risk area à la Jones, Day?

First, why are we seeking out an area of opportunity when we are already so busy. And as a corollary shouldn't we stop taking new business and consolidate what we have?

It is interesting to note that this very valid question is usually raised by younger members of the partnership. There is obviously a reason for that. We are the product of our own experience. If one has only known boom times in the practice of law and one's principal concern is how to get the work done—then naturally you wonder why management is exacerbating that problem by aggressively involving the firm in new areas of the law.

On the other hand, if you are a World War II person who was raised with dinner conversation concerning the Depression years, have gone through periods where the only practice you had was what you brought to the firm, and have gone through days when the department was dead in the water with no growth in sight, then you worry about how to keep this huge machine busy during the next down cycle, which you are sure will come.

I worry about adequate workload from three viewpoints—(1) if we should have a material and lengthy drop in our workload—the chain reaction this would cause in professional morale if we do not have quality work to keep our lawyers busy, (2) the blow to our young lawyers because of the lack of professional growth and opportunity for partnership, and (3) the effect of the drop in profitability, particularly as this would affect our young lawyers.

We have no reason to believe that cycles are not with us in our profession, as well as in business as a whole—or that we could not lose whole areas of business by external factors such as dramatic statutory changes in important areas of the law or in litigation procedures. That is why those in governance are driven to seize opportunity—but always within our philosophic framework and policies. The older partners have also learned from experience that opportunities do not lie around for very long just to be picked up at one's convenience. That is why it is a very basic tenet of the executive committee and management committee to be opportunistic—today—every day—to get the long lead time started on new projects.

When there are new faces in governance, they could well look at this differently. We cannot.

The next question relates to whether the firm should undertake new opportunities if this means the lateral entry of a partner or associates.

Here again the answer of those involved in strategic planning of the firm is based on their own experience. The answer is yes—if we can find the right person to exploit the opportunity. The percentage of lateral entry into the partnership is very small in the overall picture—and to date has been an outstanding success in every way. As to the lateral hiring of associates, this subject is a difficult and complex matter. Next Monday night a dinner meeting of the law school committee will review this subject. I hope that a broad consensus will follow. I might say that here again, communication is a major problem. We need to do a better job in telling our associates as to what is going on and why. It appears that the communication problem might well be a more serious problem than the lateral hiring program itself. Advance notice.

Another question—are we moving so fast that we may lose the traditional identity of Gibson, Dunn & Crutcher?

Last year I tried to answer the question as to who we are. My description was as follows:

A steadily growing *old western* law firm providing high-quality, sophisticated legal services on a national and international basis.

Although its ninety-one-year history is not old in an Eastern Seaboard sense, it is *very* old in the history of Southern California. This means tradition—ties to the community, its history, its culture—pride in what we have achieved.

Although old in years—young in nature. By this I mean we are aggressive, opportunistic, and hardworking.

By "western" I said I meant that we are informal and not stratified. By the fact that the firm is growing, I indicated that this meant to me opportunity—mobility. A young lawyer does not have to wait for a death in order to achieve high rank in the firm.

I believe that the above description fits the firm today—namely—tradition—ties to the past and to the firm—pride—informality—opportunity and mobility. It would seem to me that there is more opportunity now than ever.

Question: Does our overall concept put us in a danger zone à la Jones, Day, or Seyfarth, Shaw?

As I understand the Jones, Day situation, it was the autocratic rule from Cleveland without consultation or communication that lead to the breach. The Seyfarth, Shaw problems appear to relate to helter-skelter growth and serious difficulties in the transition of governance and in financial planning.

One of our highest priorities is consulting and communicating with our branch offices on a regular and systematic basis, as well as informally. We meet separately and we meet together. We work very hard at trying to make everyone feel that this is one firm. That is the purpose of the branch partners meetings and the interoffice visiting. We truly do value the opinions of those in the branches. We truly do communicate with them and seek their views. For these reasons we hope that we are not repeating the errors of Jones, Day. Nothing would disappoint those in governance more than to have such an event occur.

As to Seyfarth, Shaw, we believe that our growth is controlled and planned, and within our traditional guidelines. And our financial position is extremely strong.

But don't get me wrong. Although we hope we are avoiding these problems, we are anything but smug about them, and very very sensitive to these issues.

In conclusion, I think that all of the evidence available indicates that this great firm at the close of its ninety-first year is doing very well. I believe that we could grow at almost any rate we desire. We have chosen to lead a restrictive course—although it might not seem like that to some—that still takes advantage of the opportunities within our master plan, but does not breach our philosophy of growth from within. We recognize that the pressures of the workload are enormous—we hope that with the success of our recruiting program, these pressures will abate to more reasonable levels over the next several years.

This is a period of transition in the leadership side of the governance of the firm. The immediate post–World War II generation of partners are now in their sixties or fast approaching. It is time to think of succession and to plan for the balance of this century. This retreat is an important step in that direction.

I thank you for listening to me.

Appendix B3. 1982 Retreat Speech by F. Daniel Frost

This is the ninety-second year of the great law firm of Gibson, Dunn & Crutcher.

I bring special greetings and wishes to you hard-nosed partners from Max Bleecher. After receiving a warm response from the business community to Max's comments, we have been thinking of giving him the 1982 Gibson, Dunn & Crutcher award for the person who has contributed the most during the year to the prestige of the firm.

This has certainly been the year of publicity for GD&C. During this calendar year major articles have appeared in the *American Lawyer*, the *National Law Journal*, and the *New York Times*. Much of this interest, of course, is attributable to our alumni in the government. On balance, I think we have come out fairly well with all of our constituencies, except perhaps the law schools with regard to the *New York Times* article, although there are mixed reports even there. Nevertheless, our relations with the media are always of great concern because one never knows what judgment call is going to be made by the writer. However, since we believe in and, I might add, vigorously and profitably defend the First Amendment for many of our clients, it is obvious that the spotlight from the media is something we will just have to live with as gracefully as possible—although it is not a comfortable experience. Perhaps being on the receiving end of this experience will make us better prepared to understand our nonmedia clients when they go through the same ordeal.

Let's take a current reading of the legal profession and of our firm in particular.

First of all, I think we must realize that despite the stock market, the economy in general is in very bad condition—much worse than the media or government pronouncements state. From recent board meetings, discussions with senior management of a number of companies and from confidential economic reports of several major investment banking firms, it is clear the decline in business activity has continued. Far from bottoming out in the spring as the administration and most private analysts had expected, the economy weakened further during the summer months. Since economic activity appears to have relapsed again in Europe and may be about to do so in Japan, the whole world economy is still in the grip of the worst recession since the Great Depression. Although the unemployment rate has not changed too much recently, other data show a marked deterioration in labor market conditions. There are no signs yet of the consumer spending surge that had been widely anticipated.

The most recent developments in the economy have been rather ominous. Especially disturbing has been the explosive rise in initial claims for unemployment benefits. During the month of August, initial jobless claims were at the highest in this recession. Because the initial claims figures provide a good index of new layoffs, they signify a dramatic deterioration in labor market conditions.

Other economic indicators also show a weakening in activity. The Fed's industrial production index fell again in August and early September as did retail sales and housing starts. Further, there are also signs of renewed declines abroad.

In this context, the worst economy since World War II, I think it is remarkable that the firm has done as well as it has. As you know, we budgeted a little over $1,500 per new share for 1982. Although our revenue is down from budget, our actual costs are also below budget. Thus our net income is very close to budget for the nine months ended September 30. The budget process provides a good discipline both in its preparation and in post mortem. There is no question but that under Dick Carncross's leadership, we are becoming much more sophisticated in the budget process. However, despite the fact that 1982 might well be our second-best year ever, there is no room for complacency or even confidence until we receive a strong signal from reliable sources that we are truly out of the recession. We are now trying to walk that difficult line of planning for both an economic deterioration and an economic upturn. When the recovery does come, we want to be ready. In the meantime we will try to hunker down as much as possible—in the event the economy gets even worse than it is now. We must take the economy into account in all that we do.

Nineteen-eighty-two has been a traumatic year for the legal profession. The combination of rising costs and a difficult economy has accomplished what has apparently never occurred before—the dissolution of three well-known middle-sized firms, (1) Kaplan, Livingston, (2) Greenbaum Wolf and (3) Marshall Bratter, and the reduction in the size of other firms such as Kutak. And for every firm whose troubles are known, there must be many who have escaped publicity. By coincidence, we are aware of Bracewell Patterson's woes. I have heard that Shephard Mullin have closed their branch in Century City and that Meserve Mumper is splitting up. Some of us know how desperate things got at Willis Butler before the split up. There are rumors about Kindel & Anderson. And so forth.

We are very familiar ourselves with the difficulties caused by rising costs and a troubled economy. The slow payment of bills by some clients, or even bankruptcy in some cases, causes a serious disruption in cash flow. Fortunately, our broad client base and diversification have softened these blows. Also we are fortunate—just plain lucky—that our Washington office had not become deeply involved in the regulatory practice before the recent deregulation movement.

Not only has 1982 been a traumatic year for the legal profession, but the future could hold dangerous times for it. Coupled with the bad economy, it is a period of transition from a cottage industry to one in which technology, skillful management, and the business aspects of the practice are becoming more and more important. One can regret the change, but it would be foolish to try to turn back the course of events that has overcome middle-sized and large firms. I believe it is possible for a sole practitioner, or a very small firm, to practice as they choose—but once one enters the main arena of large city practice representing substantial clients, there is no alternative.

A recent article in the *Legal Times* of Washington blamed a lack of strategic planning as the principal reason for the problems I have mentioned. But an analysis of what the author meant by strategic planning covers the whole field of law firm management including the recruiting, development and training of lawyers, the development of clients, the business and financial side of a firm, and long-range planning. We have talked about these matters at the last two retreats. At the very least we can say that we have identified the problems and have been working on them for some six to seven years.

In 1980 I predicted the disappearance of some large firms and the merger of others. I was correct on the first point and not on the latter. So far as I know, the merger of two large firms has not yet occurred, although there have been a substantial number of mergers of large and middle firms with smaller firms. Most of these mergers have been accomplished in a very quiet way with little publicity. I still think that large mergers will occur, as firms grope for answers to the financial problems they are facing.

In 1981 I talked about business cycles, and indicated that although we were then in a strong economy we did not expect that trend to continue indefinitely. In making those comments, I had no idea as to how soon that prediction would occur. Being an optimist, I have hopes that the economy will improve in 1983 (although I believe it will be a very slight improvement), and that 1984 will be fairly strong. However, there are some forecasters who are saying that our economy will never get back to the boom times we have known in the past unless it is led by the housing and automobile industries. And they express doubts that those two industries will ever return to what we have known before. Thus it might be the scenario during the balance of this decade that our economy will be in a state of stagflation as has been the case in Europe for some years now. If so, we will continue to have to work and plan even harder than before in order to maintain our profitability. On the other hand, as I have mentioned, we must also be positioned for a major upturn, if this should occur.

Last year I mentioned that we felt the reasons for opening the San Jose office, to have access to the venture capital business and the high technology industry, would be helpful in strengthening the firm. From every reading that I get and from talking to my fishing friend Pitch Johnson, one of the best in the field, venture capital and high technology might well be two of a handful of areas of the economy that have been proven to be recession resistant. That is another situation in which luck has proven to be more important than good planning. Last year I also made the remark that we would probably not have a New York office by 1985. I mentioned the reluctance of some members of the firm to open a New York office unless it could be full service. As you know, within the last ninety days we have rethought that conclusion and decided we should institute a toehold office in New York City beginning with a real estate practice. As of today, it appears that this office will open on November 1 at One Park Avenue Plaza. I believe this change in direction is a good example of how a long-range plan should constantly be reviewed as circumstances change. I think the decision is a correct decision, and that one, five, and ten years from now, we will be increasingly pleased that we are in New York.

I have talked a lot over the past several years about the desirability— indeed the necessity—for the firm to be represented in the Far East. During 1982 we have worked vigorously to try to assist governmental and private efforts to open Japan for foreign lawyers. Although there was some ray of hope during the summer, I am becoming increasingly skeptical that this will occur during this decade. That does not mean that we will lessen our efforts, but it is obvious we must look to the alternatives of Hong Kong or Singapore. However, because of the high cost of opening an office in either locality, I am inclined to think that our current procedure should be one of watchful waiting and moving only when the right opportunity occurs. I have not yet seen the right formula of personnel and clients to indicate a profitable operation in Hong Kong or Singapore after one year—our traditional formula.

In the meantime our onshore efforts to increase our representation of Japanese clients in the United States has been remarkably successful.

I mentioned last year that during the week following the retreat, the management committee would have its first meeting with the newly elected advisory committee. I said we expected a great deal from this committee. This expectation has been more than fulfilled. In my view, one of the truly outstanding management changes that has recently occurred was the creation of the advisory committee. We have given the committee a number of difficult assignments, and in every case have received thoughtful and wise responses. In turn the advisory committee has made a number of suggestions to the management committee which have been very helpful. I am hopeful that the role of the advisory committee can be expanded even further in the future.

Lastly, during the 1981 retreat we worried about whether the firm was growing too fast. As you all know, the latest survey published in the *Legal Times* of Washington indicated that we are now the sixth-largest law firm in the United States. Although we have never sought growth as such, or based any of our strategic planning on how many lawyers we could employ, it is nevertheless of interest that our planning has achieved such a result. Information since that date has indicated to us that our growth is at about the same rate as our main competition, for example, O'Melveny & Meyers and Pillsbury, Madison & Sutro. It is slower than those who have merged with other firms, such as Latham and Watkins, Rosenman, Colin, etc. In this regard I was pleased to note that we are not one of the twenty fastest-growing firms in the United States. To me this means that our growth has been controlled, and achieved primarily internally. This is not true of many of the firms listed in the twenty fastest growing. I am sure you all noted in the article in the *Legal Times* as to the numerous mergers that have occurred. The hard fact is that the largest firms are growing rapidly. Perhaps that is one of the reasons the middle-sized firms are having so much difficulty.

I would like to make one more remark as to our standing vis-à-vis other firms as to size. I do not believe that we will exceed our current ranking, because most, if not all, of the firms above us have indicated a willingness to merge with other firms. In fact, we will probably slip back in standing because I expect firms smaller than our firm to merge with others. I don't want anyone to be disappointed about this when it occurs.

Now let us take a look at this firm on this eighth day of October 1982. In 1980 in an effort to verbalize who we are, I described our firm as follows: "A steadily growing old western law firm providing high-quality, sophisticated legal services on a national and international basis."

I mentioned that we are old in years but young in nature. Obviously old is a relative term. Ninety-two years is not old in many parts of the country, but in Los Angeles it certainly is. I have noted from the biography of I. N. Van Nuys by Jim Page that the population in Los Angeles in 1900 was 120,000, and this was ten years after the firm was founded.

The fact that the firm is old means that it has traditional ties to and pride in the past. By the term "western," I mean that the firm is informal and not stratified. By young in nature I mean that it is aggressive, opportunistic, and hardworking. The term "growing" means opportunity and mobility. The fact that we have moved from a regional to a nation and international firm and practice sophisticated law means that we are in the forefront of the legal practice.

I believe that this description equally fits the firm today.

Now let us look at some of the particular problems facing our firm. I feel, and I realize that this is a judgment call, that we do not have enough people at the younger and middle partnership levels to meet the needs of the firm and demands of our clients. It is there that the great load of the work of the firm rests, as well as the primary responsibility for teaching younger lawyers. It is understandable why we are understaffed in those age brackets. These are lawyers who have been with the firm some ten to twenty years. Ten to twenty years ago the firm was not planning for what we have now become. It seems to me that the partnership must face this issue. I am inclined to doubt that the firm will be able to compete in growth with the major firms in this country unless we can more rapidly increase the number of people with experience and excellence to handle major assignments on their own, either through the rapid maturation of our more senior associates and/or the lateral association of additional partners. The problem becomes very acute to all of those who try to staff the work of the firm on a day-to-day basis. San Jose has been woefully undermanned almost from the beginning, although now we are doing much better. Los Angeles has been sending excellent lawyers into other offices for years. As you know, these problems have been exacerbated by the loss of Larry Calof and Woody Godbold, but I think we must recognize that such losses will occur periodically, either to government or industry. Somehow we must provide the firm with enough younger and middle-level partners to survive these permanent and temporary changes in career, and yet be able to take care of our client load and the growth of the firm.

Another problem I see is our need to give a more stable continuing business base to our overseas offices. Improvement is being made all the time, but the workload in those offices still fluctuates too much because of the transaction nature of the engagements.

In addition we must constantly improve our quality control. Obviously the whole future of the firm rests on our ability to provide high-quality legal services.

Another area of improvement is to do a better job at communicating both at the partnership and associate level. As hard as we try, it does not seem possible to do enough in this area. One assistance we will soon have is the auditorium at the Crocker Center, which will allow us for the first time to have a single meeting with all of our Los Angeles associates in one room. We must constantly work at keeping our sense of collegiality that we have always had. We must seek to have our associates fully understand the opportunities that are available to them because of the growth of the firm. This only occurs through communication.

It is my understanding that a poll of the participants in our own summer program shows a criticism of it for various reasons. This is something that we are examining very carefully.

On the positive side of things, I think we really have to keep in context that the partners of the firm have fared very well in a financial sense. I have recently had given to me a survey of the 1981 average salary levels for the top legal officers in companies with $1 billion in sales or more, both from a California viewpoint and a national viewpoint. These compensation levels include both salary and bonus. They indicate a California average level of $105,000 and a national level of $120,000. Even adding on the perks for retirement pay, cars, etc., you can see that the financial rewards in the firm are very good.

By the end of this year we should be moving into the Crocker

Center. I am advised by the senior management of Crocker, and also by John Cushman and Rob McGuire, that the first tower should be 92 percent rented by the time we move in. It is interesting to note that the deal struck by IBM in the second tower was for a 20 percent equity interest in exchange for renting 50 percent of the space at a cost of $20 million. And the rent is at $30 per square foot. If IBM with all of its muscle obtained that kind of a deal, it makes us all the more appreciative of our 15 percent interest for initially renting 150,000 square feet out of approximately 1,300,000 square feet (about 11 percent) and our rental is about $19.60 per square foot. Ralph Wintrode tells me that we should be paying off our loan for the move and the investment—a total debt of about $3.1 million borrowed from the Crocker partnership to pick up our deficit capital—in approximately six years. This seems incredible—but is based upon an actual rental schedule which will generate cash income to us in 1985 of about $1.5 million and $2.4 million by 1986 (plus the Arco payments). In 1989 the firm should be receiving $3.6 million from the building and $720,000 from Arco, with no debt.

We are very much aware that we are getting closer to the celebration of our centennial. Thanks to Bruce Toor we now have dozens of tape recordings of people who are familiar with the history of our firm. In addition we pretty well know now what is in our files in the way of historical data. I am hopeful that all of this information can be put together into an exciting book by a professional writer. This is a sentimental project that you can be sure we will give a high priority during the balance of this decade.

In summary, I think it is fair to say that we are holding a steady course on our long-range plan, and that the firm will probably have its second-best year ever in an absolutely disastrous economy. We are trying to balance caution and growth to be able to respond to the different economic scenarios we foresee as possible during the balance of this decade. And whether we like it or not, we are in the spotlight as to everything we do, especially if we make mistakes or perceived mistakes. Hopefully this situation will fade away as time passes.

This retreat is devoted to the subject "Gibson, Dunn & Crutcher—

a Business." I am confident that we will all learn a lot about that aspect of ourselves during the next two days. Although I am convinced that it is the economic success of the firm that must receive our first priority, we must never lose sight of the fact that close behind are many human factors that also must receive our most serious and constant attention.

I thank you.

Appendix B4. 1984 Retreat Speech by F. Daniel Frost

My fellow partners, welcome to the partners retreat in this ninety-fourth year of the great law firm of Gibson, Dunn & Crutcher.

Before beginning, I would like to extend a very warm welcome to those partners who are at their first partners retreat, and to our special guest, and former partners, Ted Olson. Ted has just been reelected to the partnership and will join our Washington, D.C., office on November 1.

I would also like to give special recognition to our excellent administrative directors, Kathy Kennedy and Dick Carncross. As the firm has grown larger they have had to work at a frantic pace to keep up. I feel they have performed heroically under difficult circumstances. Under their guidance the quality of our administrative services has become better and better even though the burdens have become more intense.

We are also very fortunate to have Harry Hufford with us during the retreat. As you all know, Harry will join the firm on January 7, 1985, as chief administrative officer to work with Kathy and Dick in administering the firm during the years to come. We are extremely fortunate to have Harry, since all who know him consider him to be the ultimate professional manager, as well as a man of enormous tact and integrity. His training under five supervisors who have one common trait, great egos, has given him an excellent background for Gibson, Dunn & Crutcher. We are also giving careful consideration to the possibility of asking Harry to assist the firm in two additional areas—(a) our expanding efforts in the field of health care, and (b) in city, county, and state relations for our clients.

Since it appears there will not be a partners retreat in 1985, and thus, this is the last time I will be addressing a retreat of the partnership as chairman of the management committee, I thought it would be timely to give an accounting. In effect this accounting will describe what has occurred during the watch of my generation in management, being the twenty-three-year period 1962 to 1984. Obviously the figures you will hear and look at are attributable to the efforts of all of the lawyers in the firm over that time span. However, I personally feel particularly obligated to those partners, who cover a broad age spectrum, who have labored so hard in supporting and carrying out our expansion program starting in 1977.

It was in 1962 that the generation of current senior lawyers in the firm first achieved management status. It seems only a few years have passed since we were considered the young turks. The charts I am going to show you were not able to cover more than the twenty-year period of 1964 to 1983. Thus, I thought I would make a few off-chart remarks as to 1962 and 1963.

In 1962, according to the P-W report for that year, the firm had 64 lawyers, 32 partners, and 32 associates. As usual in a P-W report, this figure is a weighted average of the year for what P-W calls lawyer equivalents. Although our partner-to-associate ratio was 1 to 1, the median ratio on a national basis was about 2 associates to 1 partner.

In 1963 we had 66 lawyers—34.5 partners and 31.5 associates, an inverse ratio.

Our gross income for 1962 was $3,803,000, and for 1963 was $4,281,000. As you know, our current monthly overhead is about $4.8 million, larger than our entire gross income for 1963. Our gross revenues this year will be approximately $100,000,000.

The management committee has been in existence for about six years, starting in 1979. It was originally composed of three of the more senior partners of the firm. However, it has gradually evolved and now covers a twenty-year age span within the partnership—a very healthy and important development. The management committee has had primary responsibility for the management of the firm beginning in 1979. In the accounting to follow I will give particular attention to that period, using 1979 as a base year.

I am now going to present a series of charts which will depict in graphic form what has happened to the firm during the past twenty years, 1964 to 1983.

The first chart shows you in bar form the growth in the number of lawyers, broken down between associates and partners, with the index on the right-hand side. It also has a curve indicating the associate-partner ratio during this period of time, with the index on the left.

Lawyers	Ratio
1964—71	1964—1.09
1969—104	1969—1.26
	1970—1.88
1974—152	1974—1.20
	1977—.91
1979—200	1979—1.08
	1983—1.52
1984—Today 391	

In all cases, P-W figures are being used (see charts pp. 178–182).

You will note a temporary aberration in the associate-partner ratio in 1970 when it reached 1.88 to 1 for a brief period. This was caused by the fact that we added twenty-three associates in that year, and the number of partners declined by three due to deaths and retirements. At the end of the year 1970 we elected ten associates to partnership, and the ratio immediately dropped to 1.4 to 1. The ratio continued to drop until in 1977 and 1978 it was less than 1 to 1. Starting in 1979, the ratio began to rise. In 1983 it was 1.52 to 1. Today the ratio is 1.66 to 1, including only those members of the class of 1984 who are aboard. If we include all of the class of 1984, the ratio is 1.75 to 1.

The next chart depicts average partner income during the twenty-year period. Note the steep increase starting in 1979. 1979—$170,844; 1983—$256,167. For 1984, the result will probably exceed $275,000.

This chart is an overlay of chart 2 on chart 1. It is interesting to note the parallel growth of API [annual profitability index] with the increase in the ratio starting in 1979.

We now have a chart depicting EPS [earnings per share] for the twenty-year period. Note again the steep rise starting in 1979. 1979—

$1,201, 1983—$1,800. In 1984, EPS will probably exceed $2,000 per share—thus off the chart.

This chart is an overlay of EPS on the first chart. Again the significant factor is the steep rise since 1979 as the ratio has increased.

Here we have a chart depicting gross and net income for the twenty-year period—and the steep curve for 1979 to 1983 stands out again. 1979—gross $35,054, net $16,401; 1983—gross $77,842, net $32,277.

Here we have imposed the gross and net income chart on the first chart. I think it speaks for itself.

Lastly, we have the financial results for the first nine months of 1982, 1983, and 1984.

What can we derive from these charts:

1. You noted that the associate-partner ratio has been all over the map. During the twenty years the ratio reached 1.88 to 1 in 1970 for a very brief period of time before the year-end decisions as to partnerships, and then declined rapidly over the next seven years to below a 1 to 1 ratio in 1977 and 1978. Only in 1979 did it get back to a positive ratio, and this has steadily risen the past five years.

2. During the long slump in the ratio from 1971 through 1978, API and EPS did steadily rise, but not equal to inflation. The reverse has been true since 1979. According to the 1983 P-W survey, our API was up 13 percent over inflation in the 1979 to 1983 time frame, whereas the median for the firms in both the national and California surveys did not keep up with inflation. In fact, in the California survey, median income per partner in 1983 was 83.3 percent in 1979 on an inflation adjusted basis. In 1984 we are running strongly ahead of inflation and thus the 13 percent should increase substantially.

3. Since the base year 1979, API and EPS have both increased by about 50 percent through 1983, and in 1984 it appears that both API and EPS will take another hefty jump.

I really do not want to make too much of these figures. They obviously show a very profitable firm with the trends going in the right direction. I am not trying to make the point that the improvement in the profitability of the firm has been caused solely by the change in the ratio. Obviously there have been many other contributing factors, such as the increase in the quality of our legal engagements, which, in turn, has allowed us to steadily increase our billing rates. And it is not a coincidence, in my opinion, that the increase in the quality of our legal engagements ties in time sequence to our multioffice expansion program.

Even though I do not want to overemphasize the associate-to-partner ratio, I can assure you that if the firm were to hire a management consultant, they would pound on the importance of the ratio from morning to night. I have heard them do it time and again at various symposiums.

We have been giving real attention to achieving our goal of improving profitability each year per share—the short-term problem—and yet to also position the firm for the future. It is your management's view that the glue that holds this and all other law firms together can be said to be composed of collegiality, the firm culture, constant communication, and profitability—and probably the most important of these ingredients is profitability. This might be a cynical view—but history bears out the fact that if the net profits of a firm drop, over a period of time, the firm begins to have problems.

Thus, we are particularly proud of our financial results in that they were achieved during a period when we were incurring substantial costs in order to position ourselves on a national and international basis. We have not stinted in these expenditures. All of our physical facilities are of the highest quality—most of them almost brand new. We keep our books on the same basis as we file our tax returns—we amortize leasehold improvements, for example, over the shortest period allowed. We capitalize as little as possible. Thus, the balance sheet is very clean. Yet with these heavy current costs to position ourselves for the future, we still have been able to enjoy record net income per share and record average partner income.

I think that the firm has done a remarkable job in projecting costs, and in general, in cost control—although improvement is always being sought. However, in understanding these rising costs, one must also understand that in the legal profession generally they are rising faster than inflation. This is primarily due to the increase in occupancy costs and in salaries for support staff. When this is understood and controlled to the greatest extent possible, one looks to the possible increase in revenues in order to sustain profitability or, hopefully, even increase it.

I know everyone here recognizes that there are basically only three ways to increase revenues in a law firm: (a) a greater number of chargeable hours per attorney, (b) higher billing rates, which is particularly obtainable through an increase in the quality of legal engagements, and (c) a higher ratio of associates to partners.

I would now like to turn to some slides relating to our balance sheet.

The first shows a calculation of working capital—in the traditional sense the difference between current assets and current liabilities. You will note that our working capital has increased in the period 1979 to 1983 at basically the same percentage as the increase of attorneys, revenues, and net income. It might astonish some of you to see that we have about $43 million in working capital. This should be distinguished from what we call free cash, which excludes receivables and unbilled time. Frankly, we are not pleased with this figure. Obviously, it directly reflects the lag between work done and payment received. To the extent it can be reduced—the reduction drops to the bottom line as profit.

Now let's look at the equity position of the partnership. Taking the Crocker Center at depreciated book value of $1,551,000, at 12/31/83, the equity was $47,172,000. As you know we have elected to report our gain on the Crocker Center on the installment basis. The total sales price as about $7.2 million, almost all of which was gain. We were able to achieve this sale even though the terms of our lease with Arco did not give us the right to keep the appreciation. Fortunately for us, Arco wanted us out very badly.

Please note that fixed assets, basically leasehold improvements and equipment, after amortization and depreciation, amount to about $6 million. I also want to call attention to the fact that retirement and death benefits have not been booked—simply because we would not know what to book. Thankfully the Crocker Center investment at least partially offsets that liability, as Bob Burch will report on in detail Sunday morning.

I think that is enough of a financial analysis.

I would now like to turn to a review of the legal profession in general.

As is well known, no net new job formation has been made by the Fortune 500 Industrials during the past four years, during which the American economy has created some 4 million net new jobs. The increase has come about through greater emphasis in our economy on personal services, as well as the increasing importance of small and middle-size businesses. As the economy has shifted from depending primarily on a large industrial base to service industries and smaller companies, this has required law firms to also change their areas of emphasis away from the large industrial companies to providing services for smaller companies and the service industry. In order to survive, law firms have had to give increasing emphasis to the shifting areas of specialization. As an example, the area of real estate financing, development, and related activities has grown faster than the economy as a whole. This area of our economy has a vociferous appetite for legal services since many, if not most, of the companies involved are not large enough to have established a self-sufficient internal legal department.

A similar example is the financial services industry, which is restructuring itself and growing at an enormous rate.

Two distinct types of specialization have emerged. The first is pure and simple legal specialization, the specialization in the technical aspects of existing and emerging law. The other specialty could be called a functional specialization, such as in health care, financial services, venture capital, and the like. These functional specialties use a whole spectrum of legal services in the classic sense, such as tax, litigation, labor, corporate work, and so forth. It is in these areas that the large law firms have a distinct advantage. They can supply a broad coverage of the legal specialties to service a functional specialization and they can do it in depth and they can do it on a geographic basis if the firm has branches.

Branches, in turn, have changed the legal profession. It is my understanding that only two of the largest fifty firms do not now have branches—the two being Jenner & Block and Covington, Burling. Even those firms that a few years ago pooh-poohed the idea of branches, are now reconsidering the whole issue. As you know, Sullivan & Cromwell either soon will, or already has, opened an office in Los Angeles. Davis Polk will soon follow, it is rumored. Skadden, Arps has taken an extremely aggressive approach to its geographic expansion, to say nothing of Finley, Kumble; this change in the legal profession has been noticed by not only the journals serving the profession, but also by the *New York Times* and the *Wall Street Journal* . . . .

Up until recently it was pretty well accepted that there are two basic models for law firm management and strategic planning. The first model is that exemplified by some of the most successful New York firms that had reached a desired size eight to ten years ago, usually about 200 lawyers, and had made a conscious decision not to grow, except in a very limited manner. As a part of this policy has been a decision that in order to keep the profitability of the firm, there would have to be an extremely tight control over the admission to partnership. Typically, there would be one or two admissions to partnership from a class, but sometimes none. These firms did not have difficulty in recruiting associates, because of their historic reputation within the legal profession, their blue chip client base, and their outplacement program for associates who did not become partners. This model requires the strictest of discipline to enforce a rigid quota system. The firms are admittedly run for the benefit of the partners with a very cold view towards the aspirations of associates.

The other classic model has been the firm that has understood the economic realities of the associate-to-partner ratio; because the management of the firm has decided that growth is important to obtain the desired positioning on a national basis, the firm has been able to allow admission to partnership based upon merit and not upon a quota system. Even so, in order to reach the desired profitability, those firms have had to put in substantial chargeable hours, both at the associate and partner level.

To my knowledge there has never been an economically successful middle-size or large firm that has adopted a program of no growth and yet open admission to partnership.

I mentioned earlier that this was the traditional view of looking at the legal profession. In the last year or so it is apparent that several of the leading New York firms that had adopted a no-growth program for a number of years, such as Cravath, Sullivan & Cromwell and Davis Polk, have decided to expand their firms, not only numerically, but also at least as to Davis Polk and Sullivan & Cromwell, to reach out and establish one or more branch offices.

However, the interesting aspect of this change in direction is that, so far as one can tell, they have not changed their policy as to admission to partnership. Although adding many new lawyers, during the past year each of these firms have added only one or two partners. In other words, they are seeking the advantages of growth, without giving up the advantages of a very high associate-to-partner ratio. Obviously, such ratio will increase as the base of associates increases.

I believe that this change in direction is caused by the recognition of the following factors: (a) as I mentioned earlier, that costs in the legal profession are rising at a much faster rate than inflation, and thus law firms need to expand their revenue base, and (b) that there are markets being secured by other firms they might lose out on if they do not expand. As our friend, Bob Crandall, has said: Growth and profitability depend on holding down costs and reaching into new markets. That is true both for the airline industry and legal profession.

In any event, the concept of growth by the largest and most successful firms seems to be the order of the day. Here are some selected percentage growth rates between 1983 and 1984 that I have taken from the recent survey in the *National Law Journal*. I might add that the figures in the survey of the *Legal Times of Washington* do not exactly reconcile. However, I assume that all of the firms followed instructions, as we did—counting attorneys on hand at 6/30/84 plus the class of 1984, even if they have not yet arrived.

Paul, Hastings	32.9 percent
Hunton & Williams	27.7 percent
O'M&M	24 percent (2nd year)
Pillsbury	17 percent
Jones, Day	17 percent
Skadden, Arps	16.8 percent
Akin Gump	15.6 percent
Davis Polk	14.7 percent
Cravath	13.5 percent
Sidley & Austin	12.8 percent
GD&C	12.5 percent
Latham & Watkins	8.9 percent

If the *National Law Review Journal* figures are correct as to O'Melveny & Meyers growth, and the differential between our two firms continues into 1985, O'Melveny will be a larger firm than GD&C in the 1985 survey.

I would now like to turn to some comments on GD&C today.

At the 1980 retreat I tried for the first time to put into words what I thought would describe our firm. At that time I said that we were

"A steadily growing old western law firm providing high-quality, sophisticated legal services on a national and international basis."

This description doesn't say very much until some amplification occurs.

"Old" means tradition—ties to the history of the community—pride in the firm's achievements—an ongoing culture, folklore and heritage. (Jane Wilson has made a happy discovery—descendant of one of founders of firm, Judge Bicknell, gave to Huntington Library in 1981, a set of his letterpress books from 1874 to 1911, and files of all letters he rec'd during this period. Sheds light on development of GD&C and history of LA County. Exactly what we want for our history.)

"Western" is an extremely important word in our culture and heritage and I believe is the reason we are informal, not stratified, just plain friendly and open in our dealings with everyone in the firm.

"Growing" is very important in that it provides opportunity and upward mobility for young lawyers.

I also mentioned in 1980 that the challenge was to preserve our heritage and character—and yet to meet the challenges of the eighties.

Since the 1980 retreat we have grown a great deal. We have entered new specialties. We have opened new offices. We have learned a lot about ourselves.

I thought it might be worthwhile to list at this retreat some important additional characteristics of the firm that I feel make us different from many other firms.

I am not trying to make the point that our style, our culture, is better than that of other firms. What I think is important is that this is our culture, it is very strong, it is successful, and it is shared throughout the firm.

The first of these relates to the spirit of cooperation within the firm. Because of the increasing specialties within a firm, they increasingly contain professionals who do very different things, have very different personalities, and have very different definitions of what professionalism is. And, so it seems that it is essential for the well-being of a firm to have a spirit, as part of the culture of the firm, of mutual respect across these boundaries. Within GD&C this spirit is one of our greatest strengths. If you go to some law firms, the corporate department might not feel comfortable about the capabilities of the litigation department, or the tax department, or the labor department. So, they tend not to trust each other across these boundaries. By way of contrast, within GD&C there is an incredible mutual respect between specialties, between offices, and between the people themselves. There is a feeling that you are one of us, regardless of the fact that what you do is different or that you are a different sort of person.

I believe that this spirit is enhanced by the fact that we have one pool of profits in the firm. Although for management purposes we have detailed budgets for each office, which in turn allows us to have a consolidated budget, this budget is only a management tool and has nothing to do with the distribution of profits. No single office or department or group is a profit center for compensation purposes. Rather, there is one pool of profits for the firm as a whole, and when one partner prospers, all partners prosper; when one office prospers, all offices prosper; and when one specialty prospers, the prosperity extends to all. This in turn means that each of the offices helps each other, each of the lawyers helps each other, and each of the specialties helps the others.

Another important factor to my mind is opportunity. When talking to associates, I have always stressed something I strongly believe—the enormous opportunity for them in this firm. We have such a need for experienced lawyers, that there has developed a very fast track within the firm for those associates who have the quality of excellence and who have the ability to handle client responsibility at an early stage.

Further, this can be done within a small group—whether it is a functional group in a large office, or simply a smaller office—but with the resources and backing of a very large firm.

I believe this combination of small-group identification and large-firm support is ideal for bringing out a dynamic entrepreneurship throughout the firm, a sense of belonging, comradeship and loyalty, an early recognition of ability, and a sense of group achievement.

Another unusual aspect of our firm I have discovered in learning about other firms, is our use of committees, both regular and ad hoc, that sweeps into management a broad spectrum of partners and associates. This system is perhaps not cost effective and would be decried by many law firm managers and management advisors. Nevertheless, we think it is important and worthwhile in that it gives a sense of participation—it adds to the concept of one firm—and it is in truth deeply embedded in our culture.

A unique feature of our firm that *is* important to our economic health and stability, is our extremely broad client base. As we have seen in prior reports to the partnership, no single client contributes 5 percent of revenues—and as the revenue base gets larger, that percentage will probably decrease. And certainly the client base is increasing as we have moved into additional geographic areas.

We are also, of course, considered by our colleagues in other firms to have been at the forefront in exploiting the advantages of opening new offices. There have been a number of skeptics around, including within the firm, but now I believe the concept is widely accepted as being not only financially important but perhaps absolutely necessary for market share.

What our colleagues are not fully aware of is the tremendous synergy that has come about because of the multioffices. Hardly a week goes by but that I hear of another client opportunity realized because of our geographic position.

Let us take a look at the future.

At what size would this firm be considered to have achieved full growth within our present configuration? I believe that level is at least 700 to 800 lawyers, depending on the size desired for some key offices. But just throwing some numbers out, if New York should have 75 lawyers, Washington about the same, Denver and Dallas 50 each, and so forth, one can see that 700 to 800 lawyers would not be excessive for the opportunities we have created for ourselves.

It took GD&C seventy-eight years to become a firm of 100 lawyers. It took only ten years more to reach 200 lawyers. It appears that we will be adding 100 additional lawyers approximately every two to three years until the firm has reached its maturity, whatever that figure and date may be.

It has taken the firm its entire history to date—ninety-four years—to reach $100 million in revenues. I am confident that the $200 million level will be reached by 1990—the firm's centennial year. GD&C is now not only a large law firm—it is also a big business. One has to wonder how many industrial firms in the Fortune 500 have as many officers and employees being paid $200K a year as we have in this firm. Not very many, I would guess.

Some may think that our growth is too fast. I don't believe so. Obviously our colleagues in some of the great firms in this country are on a faster growth pattern than we are. Growth is not good or bad in itself—it depends upon the purpose and how it is done. Bad growth is growth just to be the biggest firm without accomplishing anything else. Good growth, in my opinion, is the growth occurring for the purpose of upgrading the quality of the practice, broadening the client base, expanding into a new specialty, or expanding one's capability in a particular specialty, growth for the purpose of achieving strength and depth in lawyering skills, etc.

And let me make one point very clear. The fact that, in my view, we need to grow at a fairly rapid rate at this point in time does not mean that we can't change that model in the future. It is perfectly possible for any firm at some time in the future to change its model if it desires to do so. The growth model is not a Ponzi scheme. When a firm in the growth model has achieved its desired size, it might well switch to the no-growth model. However, at that time, it must change its culture and exercise a rigorous and cold-blooded attitude toward the admission to partnership. Further, this type of change requires an early warning system for associates, just as a matter of fairness.

I would lastly like to say a few words about the changing of the guard.

At a recent symposium in New York we had a discussion concerning the three levels involved in running a law firm. There is administration, there is management, and there is leadership. The etymology of the three words is amusing. "Administrator" comes from the Latin, meaning to serve. The word "manager" comes from the Old French word which means the holder of wild horses. (It is related to the word "menagerie.") The word "leader" comes from an Anglo-Saxon word meaning travel guide. Three very different roles.

I would like to focus on the leadership function for a minute. I believe a true leader is one who can portray a sense of vision so that everybody is pulling in the same direction. He gives a common purpose and provides the continuity of the culture, folklore, and heritage.

Without wanting to anticipate or take away from the debate to be held later at this retreat, I think it is clear that the partners in this firm want to feel part of a participatory society and not a closed, noncommunicating, authoritarian society. No one would choose the latter. But the mistake that can be made is to think of a law partnership as an Athenian democracy (the permanent town meeting), where everybody has to participate in resolving everything. Instead, in order to have a well-run firm, I think it is necessary to have a mechanism to elect a very few people to perform the executive function for a period of time and when elected to give them the authority so that they can put their program into action. If they are not doing a proper job, they should be replaced.

As this firm grows larger and larger, I think it is important for the managers (the holders of wild horses) to be given the authority to lead and guide the firm.

Since 1979, we have made some strides in that direction, although sometimes the feeling one gets is more like being the dean of a faculty (God forbid as Charlie Meyers would say) than being given the amount of authority that is probably necessary to carry this firm forward into the future. Only fireplug on the street and 136 dogs—Sam Butler.

At the last two retreats I have discussed in some detail my views as to the philosophy of the governance of a law firm, and that my generation in this firm would soon be retiring from participating in management. We have tried very hard to use various ad hoc groups, as well as to use our regular committees, in order to find those partners who have management skills. I have been delighted with what has occurred. Although most of the partners in this firm want to practice law and be left alone as far as management is concerned, there are some partners who are interested and who are gifted and talented managers and I know they will be called on in the future to lead this great firm.

The present composition of the management committee will continue as is until 4/1/86. At that time both AWS and I will finish our terms as members, and the executive committee will select our replacements. While the decision as to our replacements must await that time, the framework for the orderly transition of management must be set in motion much earlier. Toward that end, I intend to increasingly delegate full management responsibilities to the other members of the management committee during the next one and a half years so that they, along with the new members who replace Art and myself, can be off to a running start on 4/1/86.

The major issues that I see facing future management are these:

1. As the firm gets larger and more complex, to what extent will the partners most actively engaged in management be able to practice law?

My own view is that some degree of lawyering is important in order for the partner to be able to be effective with clients and potential clients and to have the full respect of the firm. I think it can be done by utilizing our highly professional support staff to the maximum extent.

2. How long can the firm continue its nonquota system for new partners?

As a corollary, if we follow the no-quota system, how do we otherwise meet rising costs and protect our profitability? Putting the problem another way, to what extent can we continue to increase billing rates and chargeable hours, the other revenue factors. Future managers will have to make tough decisions in this area, particularly when the growth of the firm begins to slow down.

3. What should the configuration of the firm be in the year 2000?

By this I mean its size, its scope of specialties, its geographic locations, its management structure, and the like. It is not too early to think about these matters.

4. How can the culture of the firm be continued as the firm grows and the practice of law becomes more and more specialized in lawyering disciplines, in functional groups, and geographically?

Certainly, an enormous effort at intrafirm communications will be an important part of the solution to this problem.

I am confident that these questions—these challenges—and others we cannot now foresee, will skillfully be resolved by future management—with due regard, not only to the economic factors, which are terribly important, but also to the marvelous spirit within this firm that has developed and transpired over its long history.

GIBSON, DUNN & CRUTCHER
FINANCIAL GROWTH, 1964–1984

✦ ✦ ✦

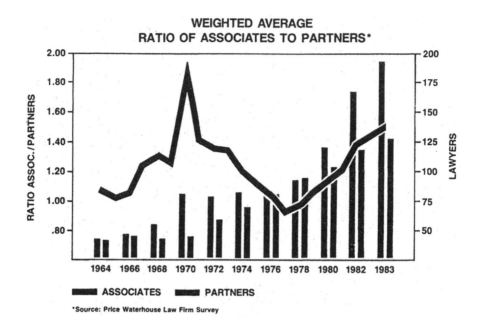

WEIGHTED AVERAGE
RATIO OF ASSOCIATES TO PARTNERS*

ASSOCIATES   PARTNERS

*Source: Price Waterhouse Law Firm Survey

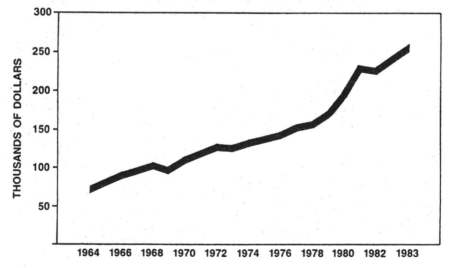

AVERAGE PARTNER INCOME

AVERAGE PARTNER INCOME

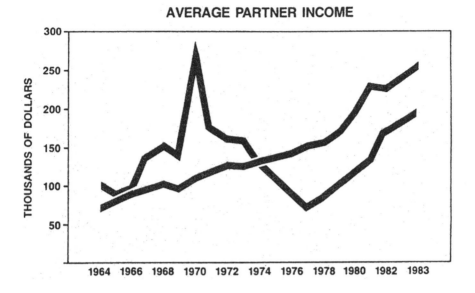

EARNINGS PER SHARE

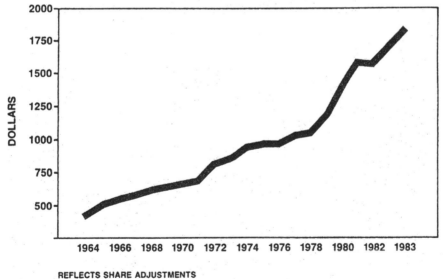

REFLECTS SHARE ADJUSTMENTS
1/1/73 AND 1/1/82

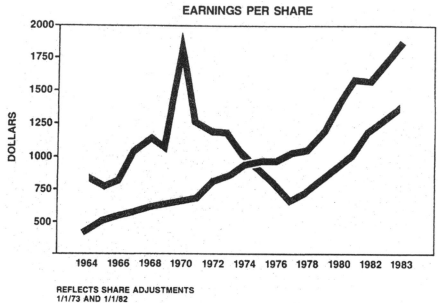

EARNINGS PER SHARE

REFLECTS SHARE ADJUSTMENTS
1/1/73 AND 1/1/82

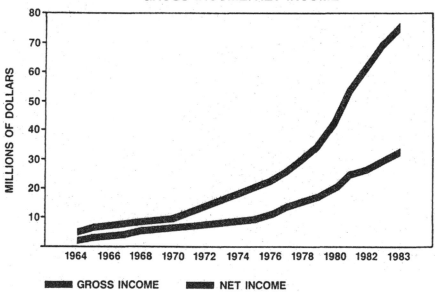

GROSS INCOME/NET INCOME

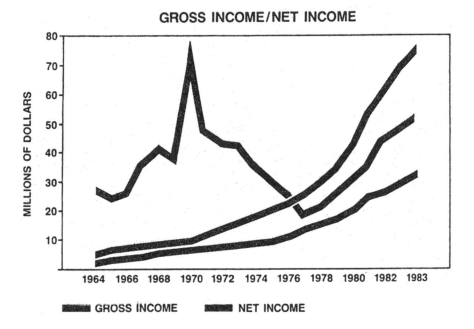

GROSS INCOME/NET INCOME

STATISTICAL DATA

	9 MONTHS ENDED SEPTEMBER 30			
	1982	1983	1984	% CHANGE 83/84
GROSS INCOME*	$46,600	$57,161	$75,004	31.2
NET INCOME*	$19,359	$23,313	$32,279	38.5
PROFIT MARGIN	41.5%	40.8%	43.0%	5.4
EARNINGS PER SHARE	$1,148	$1,302	$1,680	29.0

*Thousands of Dollars

WORKING CAPITAL
(thousands)

	1979	1980	1981	1982	1983
CASH	$1,213	$862	$1,388	$1,302	$688
BILLED AND UNBILLED FEES*	19,428	24,138	27,577	35,163	43,945
ARCO RECEIVABLE–CURRENT	–	–	–	720	720
ACCOUNTS PAYABLE	(72)	(390)	(346)	(370)	(497)
NOTE PAYABLE–CURRENT	(–)	(–)	(–)	(–)	(1,230)
DEFERRED ARCO GAIN–CURRENT	(–)	(–)	(–)	(634)	(634)
WORKING CAPITAL	$20,569	$24,610	$28,619	$36,181	$42,992

*Receivables Are Stated Gross

SUMMARY OF EQUITY
(thousands)

	1979	1980	1981	1982	1983
WORKING CAPITAL	$20,569	$24,610	$28,619	$36,181	$42,992
LONG-TERM RECEIVABLE–ARCO	–	–	–	5,200	4,480
INVESTMENT IN MAGUIRE	–	2,445	1,979	3,756	1,551
DEFERRED INTEREST/ TAXES MAGUIRE	–	–	–	1,205	1,049
FIXED ASSETS–NET	2,123	2,763	2,957	4,087	5,969
LONG-TERM NOTE PAYABLE	(–)	(2,500)	(2,500)	(6,150)	(4,920)
DEFERRED GAIN– ARCO	(–)	(–)	(–)	(4,583)	(3,949)
EQUITY	$22,692	$27,318	$31,055	$39,696	$47,172

Appendix B5. Remarks of F. Daniel Frost

"Expanding the Base by Developing New Specialties or by Branches"

American Lawyer Symposium, New York City
January 24–25, 1985.

Expanding the base by developing new specialties or expanding the base by branches can be looked on as two separate subjects, and in many ways they are. This point was forcefully argued by Sam Butler at the September seminar of the American Lawyer.

At that meeting Sam indicated he felt no pressure as to multioffices, but did agree that specialization has certainly "become the thing." He also indicated that his firm's interest and move to specialization have been within the Wall Street–type of practice.

Within that context I agree completely with Sam that specialization and multioffices can be two separate and distinct subjects.

However, outside of the Wall Street–type of practice, I believe it can fairly be stated that a move into certain areas of specialization and a multioffice system can be tied closely together and, in fact, can be mutually interdependent.

Before developing that statement a little further, I would like to add that my remarks are not intended to argue that a multioffice system is better or worse than a single office. I believe that each firm has to develop a strategic plan that fits its particular history, goals, and geographic location. The inclusion of the words "geographic location" might seem strange to you, but I don't believe it is a coincidence that most of the firms that have adopted the multioffice system and who have been the leaders in this movement either come from outside of Manhattan or if located in Manhattan are relatively new firms. The old traditional Wall Street firms have developed in an environment that is totally different than the firms leading the multioffice movement. I have a feeling it would be impossible to improve the quality across the board of the practice of some of the great New York firms. That has not always been the case for many firms located elsewhere. Another motivation for multioffice firms has been a perceived or real limitation imposed on their practice because of a downturn in the economic vitality of their traditional geographic area. For example, geographic areas affected by the downturn in the so-called smokestack industries. Thus, where a firm has its roots can be a very important feature in whether or not a multioffice system makes sense.

A strategic plan that is good for one firm—or even a necessity— might not be good and certainly not a necessity for another. However, it is interesting to observe that some of the old-line Wall Street firms are apparently rethinking their former strong views against multioffices.

Turning back to the question of increasing the base by specialization, I agree with Joe Flom's remarks at the September seminar that one of the advantages of specialization is that not only can it create a much broader client base, but also that new clients who have been attracted by such specialization might retain the firm in other more traditional areas of the practice of law. Thus, specialization has the possibility of a double payoff—it increases the client base as to the specialization, and it can increase the client base overall.

Now why do I think that the effective use of specialization might be tied to a multioffice system? I think it can be fairly argued that geographic location can detract from the ability of a firm to become a leading force in certain specialties. And, as a corollary, being located in a particular geographic area can be of great importance in entering a specialty.

An obvious but far-fetched example would be a midwestern firm wanting to get into the entertainment business. It just couldn't be done without another office. In fact, to show you how localized the entertainment practice is, it would be difficult for a downtown Los Angeles firm to become a major player in this area without a West Side office— Beverly Hills, or Century City, or Santa Monica. That's the way it is.

It seems to me it would be hard to be a leader in natural resources law (not the securities representation of large oil companies but the nuts and bolts of oil and gas practice, litigation, environmental issues, etc.) without being located where the action is—Louisiana, Texas, Colorado, etc.

I think it is more likely a firm can be a major player in the venture capital field if it is located in one of the high-volume venture capital markets—the Silicon Valley/Palo Alto area, Boston, etc.

Now it is also true that a firm can fairly ask, "Why should we be interested in these highly specialized areas of the law that might require a multioffice system?" I would agree that it is not necessary. My point is that you can't always separate the ability to practice a particular specialty from moving to a multioffice system.

In my view the management of every firm should first look around for the opportunities that are at hand for specialization—real estate law, both the lending and equity side, the health services industry, the insolvency practice, and the like. These areas of the law do seem to be present everywhere. I believe it is important to draw up a priority list of opportunities and then go after the top priority until that is accomplished. Then work down to the next item on the list.

Sometimes this will require a lateral entry into the partnership—sometimes it can be done by detaching a partner to learn all about a new area, and sometimes it might require one or more of these things plus another office. The important thing is to get at it—to think about it and to do it.

If the decision is to consider a multioffice system, I would like to share a few thoughts with you as to what in my opinion this should mean and what it should not mean.

1. It should not mean a program of a home office with one or more branches in which the branches are treated as outposts and the lawyers are second-class citizens not to be fully trusted with major engagements. In fact, I believe the word "branch" itself is just a bad word and should not be used. To me it is terribly important that everyone in a law firm understand the concept of one firm—that there should be no difference between the opening of an office, say in Washington, D.C., and adding another floor to the firm's existing facilities.

This state of mind can be achieved if there is a great deal of communication between the offices and, equally important, a great deal of intermingling of lawyers from the other offices. This can be accomplished at the management level by a lot of travel—which seems to happen anyway in the natural course of things—and through another natural process—legal engagements that involve several offices.

2. It should not mean separate profit centers for each office for compensation purposes. I believe that an accounting system that identifies each office's profit or loss for management purposes—for budget purposes—is absolutely necessary, but that this management tool should not be used for compensation.

On the other hand, a multioffice system should mean

1. One pool of profits for the entire firm in which each partner, no matter where situated, receives partnership distributions based on his or her number of shares in the one pool. This way if one office does well, all do well. If one department does well, this is shared by all. It means that the offices will freely work with each other.

2. It should mean the transfer of excellent lawyers from the old office to the new office. This is painful, but necessary in my opinion.

3. It should mean one system of awarding partnership shares—advancement in the partnership—that is the same firmwide. In other words, one standard for advancement.

4. It should mean a system of firm management that draws on lawyers from all over the firm. I am a believer in multioffice committees.

5. It should mean a program to encourage movement by associates and partners to various offices even if for limited periods of time.

6. It should mean a program that sees to it that the associates in each office know personally as many as possible of the senior lawyers in the firm. I would encourage the management of a multioffice firm to meet separately on a periodic basis with not only the partners, but even more importantly the associates in each office in informal Q&A sessions.

7. It should mean a law firm policy and culture that regard clients as clients of the firm and not of any particular partner. This will ease the question of allowing a new office to work on that clients' matters.

8. And lastly it should mean a sharing of firm culture and history through retreats, partnership, and departmental occasions, etc.

I realize that there are deep feelings in the bar that a multioffice system does not really do anything for a law firm on the theory that another office will never add to the profitability of the firm. In fact it seems to be widely shared that another office will probably be a drag on profits, and at best a wash.

And that although another office might add clients, this does not do anything for the firm as a whole—that the new clients are simply clients of the other office and not of the firm.

Again, let me say that I have no feeling of missionary zeal to convert anyone to the multioffice system. It depends on what is best for a particular firm as that firm sees it. And I don't think that missionary zeal is needed here. I have noticed that all participants but our friend from Canada represent firms with more than one office.

Assuming that a multioffice system makes sense for a firm from a viewpoint of its culture and aspirations, I have a lot of trouble understanding the thinking that another office cannot add to the overall profitability of a firm or cannot add clients to the firm as a whole and not just on a local basis.

It has been my observation that another office can add directly to the profits of a firm in the sense of creating more profits than the partners located there receive from the partnership pool, and indirectly in the sense of adding new clients to the firm as a whole. In our very simplistic method of office accounting that we use for management purposes and not for compensation purposes, I don't believe there is any office where the profit exactly equals the participation of the partners in that office. Some of the newer offices have a greater profit margin than some of the older offices. It depends to a great extent on the mix of the paralegals, associates, and partners at that office—the age of the partners, and how far along they are in the partnership. And of course, the cumulative total of the profits of every office equals the partnership pool. Thus, the pluses and minuses have to equal each other.

But the profit of a particular office is only part of the story. The real test is: what has the multioffice system done for the firm as a whole—its overall profitability, its profitability per share, its professionalism, its standing in the legal and business communities, the quality of its legal engagements?

In summary, I believe that the development of new specialties must be looked at by every firm and can be accomplished effectively in a single-office system. However, the development of specialties and the development of a multioffice system should not necessarily be looked on as two distinct subjects. In fact, to me, the main purpose to be achieved by a multioffice system is to enhance specialization and not to cover an additional geographic area. The latter follows but is not the cause for opening the particular office.

Appendix B6. Remarks of F. Daniel Frost

Philosophy of a Multioffice System

I would like to begin by giving you some thoughts as to the factors that should be looked at in deciding whether or not a multioffice system makes sense for a particular firm.

I think the starting point in this analysis is to look at the issue of expanding the base of practice. I believe it is a given in all of the literature on strategic planning for law firms that every law firm must consider—must examine—the desirability, in some cases the necessity, of expanding the base of its practice.

The reasons are obvious:

A. Security versus losing a client through merger or acquisition;

B. security versus clients' going in-house;

C. security versus changes in client loyalty;

D. security versus changes in law practice;

and

E. security versus economic factors affecting a client, or industry, or region.

Any of these factors can cause a serious drop in revenue. When this is combined with rising costs, the results can be very serious.

It is my view that there are two other important reasons to examine the issue of expanding the base:

A. Improvement in quality of practice;

and

B. improvement in overall profitability of the firm.

Assuming that it is deemed desirable to broaden the base, how does one go about it?

First of all, one can think in terms of expanding the base by specialization. Obviously, some expansion by specialization can be done without another office.

Or, one can think in terms of expanding the base by geographic expansion, as have the accounting firms.

Where should the emphasis be?

I believe that a law firm should never create separate offices just to achieve a multioffice system. The offices must have a purpose—they must be part of an overall cohesive plan. A multioffice system must be the result of a strategic plan that requires those particular offices in those particular locations to achieve the plan.

Further, it is my thesis that the principal underlying reason for a multioffice system should never be to achieve geographic coverage by itself, once a firm has covered its home base. Rather, the principal purpose for a multioffice system should be to expand the base by specialization. I believe that these two subjects—(A) a multioffice system, and (B) expanding the base by specialization—are in one sense separate, but can be tied closely together and, in fact, can be mutually interdependent.

Before developing that statement a little further, I would like to add that my remarks are not intended to argue that a multioffice system is better or worse than a single office. I believe that each firm has to develop a strategic plan that fits its particular history, goals, and geographic location. The inclusion of the words "geographic location" might seem strange to you, but I don't believe it is a coincidence that most of the firms that have adopted the multioffice system and who have been the leaders in this movement either come from outside of Manhattan or, if located in Manhattan, relatively new firms. The old traditional Wall Street firms have developed in an environment that is totally different from the firms leading the multioffice movement. I have a feeling it would be impossible to improve the quality of the practice of some of the great New York firms. That has not always been the case for many firms located elsewhere. Another motivation for multioffice firms has been a perceived or real limitation imposed on their practice because of a downturn in the economic vitality of their traditional geographic area. For example, geographic areas affected by the downturn in the so-called smokestack industries. Thus, where a firm has its roots can be a very important feature in whether or not a multioffice system makes sense.

A strategic plan that is good for one firm—or even a necessity— might not be good, and certainly not a necessity, for another. However, it is interesting to observe that some of the old-line Wall Street firms are apparently rethinking their former strong views against multioffices.

Turning back to the question of increasing the base by specialization, I would like to make the point that one of the advantages of specialization is not only can it create a much broader client base, but also that new clients who have been attracted by such specialization might retain the firm in other more traditional areas of the practice of law. Thus, specialization has the possibility of a double payoff—it increases the client base as to the specialization, and it can increase the client base overall.

Now why do I think that the effective use of specialization might be tied to a multioffice system? I think it can be fairly argued that geographic location can detract from the ability of a firm to become a leading force in certain specialties. And, as a corollary, being located in a particular geographic area can be of great importance in entering a specialty.

One obvious, but far-fetched, example would be a midwestern firm wanting to get into the entertainment business. It just couldn't be done without another office. In fact, you all know how localized the entertainment practice is. It would be difficult for a downtown Los Angeles firm to become a major player in this area without a West Side office—Beverly Hills or Century City or Santa Monica. That's the way it is.

It seems to me it would be hard to be a leader in natural resources law (not the securities representation of large oil companies but the nuts and bolts of oil and gas practice, litigation, environmental issues, etc.) without being located where the action is—Louisiana, Texas, Colorado, etc.

I think it is more likely a firm can be a major player in the venture capital field if it is located in one of the high-volume venture capital markets—the Silicon Valley/Palo Alto area, Boston, etc.

Overseas offices can have a number of advantages to a firm, such as to assist in the representation of inward-bound investments, international arbitrations, and as a very esoteric example, to specialize in Islamic banking.

Now it is also true that a firm can fairly ask why should we be interested in these highly specialized areas of the law that might require a multioffice system. I would agree that it is not necessary. My point is that you can't always separate the ability to practice a particular specialty from moving to a multioffice system.

In my view the management of every firm should first look around for the opportunities that are at hand for specialization—real estate law, both the lending and equity side, the health services industry, the insolvency practice, and the like. These areas of the law do seem to be present everywhere. I believe it is important to draw up a priority list of opportunities and then go after the top priority until that is accomplished. Then work down to the next item on the list.

Sometimes this will require a lateral entry into the partnership—sometimes it can be done by detaching a partner to learn all about a new area, and sometimes it might require one or more of these things, plus another office. The important thing is to get at it—to think about it and to do it. We call this our Research and Development Program.

If the decision is to consider a multioffice system, I would like to share a few thoughts with you as to what, in my opinion, this should mean and what it should not mean.

1. It should not mean a program of a home office with one or more branches in which the branches are treated as outposts and the lawyers as second-class citizens not to be fully trusted with major engagements. In fact, I believe the word "branch" itself is just a bad word and should not be used. To me it is terribly important that everyone in a law firm understand the concept of one firm—that there should be no difference between the opening of an office, say in Washington, D.C., and adding another floor to the firm's existing facilities.

This state of mind can be achieved if there is a great deal of communication between the offices and, equally important, a great deal of intermingling of lawyers from other offices. This can be accomplished at the management level by a lot of travel—which seems to happen anyway in the natural course of things—and through another natural process—legal engagements that involve several offices.

2. It should not mean separate profit centers for each office for compensation purposes. I believe that an accounting system that identifies

each office's profit or loss for management purposes—for budget purposes—is absolutely necessary, but that this management tool should not be used for compensation.

On the other hand, a multioffice system should mean

1. One pool of profits for the entire firm in which each partner, no matter where situated, receives partnership distributions based on his or her number of shares in the one pool. This way, if one office does well, all do well. If one department does well, this is shared by all. It means that the offices will freely work with each other. I personally believe that a formula distribution of profits—for example, giving credit for business origination—is counterproductive to a true partnership, and should not be used.

2. It should mean the transfer of excellent lawyers from the old office to the new office. This is painful, but necessary, in my opinion.

3. It should mean one system of awarding partnership shares—advancement in the partnership—that is the same firmwide. In other words, one standard for advancement.

4. It should mean a system of firm management that draws on lawyers from all over the firm. I am a believer in multioffice committees.

5. It should mean a program to encourage movement by associates and partners to various offices even if for limited periods of time.

6. It should mean a program that sees to it that the associates in each office know personally as many as possible of the senior lawyers in the firm. I would encourage the management of a multioffice firm to meet separately on a periodic basis with not only the partners, but, even more importantly, with the associates in each office in informal Q&A sessions.

7. It should mean a law firm policy and culture that regard clients as clients of the firm and not of any particular partner. This will ease the question of allowing a new office to work on that client's matters.

8. And, lastly, it should mean a sharing of firm culture and history through retreats, partnership and department occasions, etc.

I realize that there are deep feelings in the bar that a multioffice system does not really do anything for a law firm on the theory that another office will never add to the profitability of the firm. In fact, it seems to be widely shared that another office will probably be a drag on profits, and at best a wash.

And that although another office might add clients, this does not do anything for the firm as a whole—that the new clients are simply clients of the other office and not of the firm.

Again, let me say that I have no feeling of missionary zeal to convert anyone to the multioffice system. It depends on what is best for a particular firm as that firm sees it.

Assuming that a multioffice system makes sense for a firm from a viewpoint of its culture and aspirations, I have a lot of trouble understanding the thinking often expressed in seminars and in the literature that another office cannot add to the overall profitability of a firm or cannot add clients to the firm as a whole and not just on a local basis, or cannot add to the quality of practice.

It has been my observation that another office can add directly to the profits of a firm in the sense of creating more profits than the partners located there receive from the partnership pool, and, indirectly, in the sense of adding new clients to the firm as a whole and upgrading the quality of practice.

In our very simple method of office accounting that we use for management purposes and not for compensation purposes, I don't believe there is any office where the profit exactly equals the participation of the partners in that office. Some offices have greater profits, some less. Some of the newer offices have a greater profit margin than some of the older offices. It depends to a great extent on the mix of the paralegals, associates, and partners at that office—the age of the partners, and how far along they are in the partnership. And, of course, the cumulative total of the profits of every office equals the partnership pool. Thus, the pluses and minuses have to equal each other.

But the profit of a particular office is only part of the story. The real test is: what has the multioffice system *done for the firm as a whole—* its *overall* profitability, its profitability *per share*, its professionalism, its standing in the legal and business communities, the quality of its legal engagements, and so on?

In summary, I believe that, once one's home base is covered, the proper approach to a multioffice system, the principal reason to have one, is to enhance specialization and not to cover an additional geographic area. The latter follows, but it is not the cause.

I believe this approach can achieve the results I have mentioned—broadening the base of practice, improving the quality of practice, and increasing overall profitability.

✦ ✦ ✦

Wynona Peters

O'odham basketball player reigns supreme on, off court

Ryan Finley

Arizona Daily Star

Tucson, Arizona Published: 2.19.2007

Grandma heard the thump-thump-thump of the basketball, and knew little Wynona's questions were coming.

"Grandma, will you watch me?"

"Grandma, can I go shoot outside?"

"Grandma, please, can you come play with me?"

"Grandma, can we go play before dinner?"

At 6, Wynona Peters was insistent.

And even though Grandma was often busy cooking dinner or doing chores at their home in Mission View RV Park on West Los Reales Road, she always caved.

Grandma and her dark-haired, dark-eyed little shooter often lost track of time as the girl launched two-handed shots into the night.

"We would plan on going for 30 minutes, and it would end up being like two, three hours," said Verna Miguel, Peters' great-aunt, but known as her grandma. "That's about all we ever did. I enjoyed it. I knew right from the start that she was going to be a big baller."

She was right.

Peters, now a senior at Salpointe Catholic High School, is arguably the best girls' basketball player in Southern Arizona.

She also has become an expert in the Tohono O'odham tradition.

The 17-year-old is the tribe's reigning Wa:k Pow-Wow Princess and a member of the Wa:k tab basket dancers, a group that performed last July Fourth at the Smithsonian's Museum of the American Indian in Washington, D.C.

And thanks to her grandma and Tucson benefactor Dan Frost, Peters will head to college soon.

Peters would not offer any of this information without prompting. Her Salpointe classmates learned of her tribal honors only a few months ago, when she was profiled in the school's student magazine. She kept quiet about her achievements for more than three years.

"As O'odham people, we don't like to show emotion," she said. "We like to keep it inside. That's how we are."

Family unites for games

It has taken a tribe to raise Peters.

Peters lives with the 59-year-old Miguel while her mother, Vivian, works. Her father, David, is a member of the Ak-Chin tribe. He lives on the reservation, in the town of Maricopa.

The family gets together at Peters' games. At least 20 O'odham drove to Flowing Wells High School for Friday's 5A Southern Regional final. Some sat in the front row, inches from the sideline, to watch Peters play up close. Others stretched out halfway up the bleachers. Her parents sat across from the Salpointe bench, so they could keep an eye on her during timeouts.

"They're very supportive fans," Peters said. "They'll go everywhere to watch me play."

The family travels to games on money earned from operating an Indian fry bread stand outside the San Xavier del Bac Mission on Sundays.

Miguel enjoys watching her protégé most. She was a standout basketball player at St. John's Indian School in Laveen in the 1960s. When she "was too old to play," she moved back to the reservation and began to coach. It was when she coached the Redskins, a women's team that traveled to other reservations, that her great-niece discovered the sport.

"She picked it up as a baby," Miguel said. "She started playing on her own at age 4, and after that, she started playing in leagues. She's been doing that since."

Miguel, who never had children of her own, taught Peters both basketball and O'odham tradition. Peters won the Little Miss Wa:k crown at age 5 after singing a song about four children who sacrificed their lives to stop a flood. She won similar titles at ages 10 and 13.

Peters was named Pow-Wow Princess last March after a pageant that required her to display both traditional and modern O'odham talents. She's since represented the tribe at the Gathering of Nations Pow Wow in Albuquerque.

Peters performs with the basket dancers, coaches basketball at the mission school and helps teach the traditional dances and songs to younger members of the tribe. She makes room for all her commitments and sees herself as an ambassador for the O'odham.

"They're both about exposure," she said. "When I play basketball, I guess it's more exposure for me on the court. When I dance, I get more exposure for my tribe. Both of those things . . . let non–Native Americans know who I am and what I stand for."

Sponsor helps her

Peters' family extends beyond the reservation.

The once-shy girl has become a member of the Salpointe community, an exclusive group that few from her tribe have the opportunity to join. She was accepted to the school after attending grade school at the San Xavier del Bac Mission School.

Her tuition is paid for by Frost, an 85-year-old philanthropist who has long sponsored students from the mission school. Frost first met Peters when she was in sixth grade; he has since followed her academic and athletic achievements closely.

"It brings joy to me," Frost said. "There have been some great kids to come through the mission school, but Wynona is very, very special. She has that maturity and a, well, spirituality about her.

"I don't know how she does it."

Peters had to adjust to life at the private school. She was admittedly shy for most of her freshman year. Salpointe "was really hard on me," she said—but she began to come out of her shell once she made the varsity basketball team that winter.

"The first time I really felt OK was my sophomore year," she said. "I think it was because of basketball."

What basketball brought out in her, she gave back to the team.

Peters averages 16 points, 5.9 rebounds and 5.6 assists per game. She's a bright, deft passer adept at finding the open player and running the floor. She'll lead the Lancers into the 5A state tournament on Tuesday in the first round against Phoenix St. Mary's.

"She makes everything go," said Scott Moushon, the Lancers' first-year coach. "She doesn't ever get a rest, and she doesn't ever come out."

The Lancers' coach first coached Peters on a summer league team four years ago.

In one game, Peters had a chance to shoot a game-tying three-pointer but passed the ball to someone who missed the shot. Basketball-wise, the move made perfect sense. But since Peters was the team's best shooter, her young coach was furious.

"I pulled her aside afterwards and said, 'Wynona, at some point you're going to have to learn how to take over a game,' " Moushon said. "When I became the head coach here this year, that was the first thing I told her: 'You're ready.' "

College lies ahead

Those who know Peters the best paint her as a quiet, willful girl who exudes the grace befitting a Wa:k princess. She will leave the reservation soon, and basketball. A hardworking student who has a 3.2 grade-point average, she's set on attending the University of San Diego.

"I'm close to everybody on the reservation, so leaving will be hard," she said.

Peters also will give up basketball to concentrate solely on school. She plans on returning to the reservation as a pediatrician after medical school.

Frost, her benefactor, has agreed to pay for all her educational expenses. He has accounted for Peters in his will.

"Some people just know who they are," Frost said. "She has this inherent wisdom, self-confidence and leadership. Because of what she is and how she is, she can be a great leader."

✦ ✦ ✦

Preface

1. Frost also still participates in the earnings of the firm, under the firm's partnership agreement.

Chapter 1

1. Frost restarted Rickey Land & Cattle in the late 1990s and became the principal owner of a large feedlot in Hereford, Texas, and an affiliated calf operation, feeding on nearby leased wheat land until ready for the feedlot. In the modern feedlot, the diet fed to the maturing cattle is not dissimilar to that used by Thomas Rickey.

2. For a fuller account of the life of Thomas B. Rickey, see Susan Imswiler, *Thomas B. Rickey: Pioneer Nevada Cattleman* (2007) (copy on file with author).

3. William and the family sometimes spelled their name Blackbourne. According to *Webster's New World College Dictionary* (3rd ed., 1996), "Bourne" and "Burn" are interchangeable, both old medieval Scottish and English words for "stream" or "river."

4. William wrote a small book about his experiences under the name Lt. William Blackbourne. It can be found in the Bancroft Library at the University of California, Berkeley.

5. The beautiful Franciscan San Miguel Mission was founded during the late eighteenth-century period of mission building in California, on July 25, 1797, by Fr. Lasuen. At first the mission was a ranch consisting of 196,105 acres—3,710 head of cattle and 700 horses—but all of these holdings were privatized by the Spanish in 1836.

In 1812, the mission was hit by an earthquake. In 1836 it was secularized, but by 1864, according to historians, although the grounds were in disarray and the ranch privatized, the church was carefully preserved and in use. Frost's family believes that this ancient mission then became the church of many Paso Robles families, including the Blackburns.

Frost family lore holds, though perhaps apocryphally, that the small Spanish cannon in the courtyard of the mission was brought back from the battle of La Cienega by Lieutenant William Blackburn. It has been there ever since.

6. California for a brief time became a republic and later was admitted as a state.

7. See note 4.

8. Frost believes that the Blackburn adobe became a relay station for the Pony Express, and then a jail, with bayonets serving as bars on the windows. His family has a picture of the Blackburn adobe at this point in its history. When Highway 101 bypassed Paso Robles and Templeton, the Blackburn adobe was destroyed.

9. *Los Angeles Times*, June 21, 1988.

10. In all these activities, Frost's mother later was followed by her daughter Alice, who became chairman of the Pasadena Parks Commission and is memorialized by "Alice's Park," a leash-free dog park in northeast Pasadena.

11. Francis Frost did not relate the story to Frost about Thomas Rickey until after Frost's mother passed away. During her own long life—even at the end, when Frost was her legal guardian—Alice never spoke to her son about her father's legal difficulties. Frost assumes this was because Alice never knew that the Nevada Supreme Court had exonerated her father, and she did not want to criticize him.

Frost greatly regrets his mother's decision not to share this with him because he could have cleared her mind. After his mother's death, Frost himself researched the 1907 episode at the State Archives in Carson City and the State Historical Society in Reno and easily uncovered the court decision that exonerated his grandfather.

12. For a fuller account, see Imswiler's *Thomas B. Rickey*.

13. The distribution of the book Frost credits to Colonel Stan Rickey, titular head of the Rickey clan and a family historian.

14. Because Rickey was an ardent Republican and supporter of the incumbent U.S. senator, his political rivals wanted to keep Rickey's bank out of the Tonapah/Goldfield/Comstock Lode area, and sought his downfall. The prosecuting attorney in the Rickey matter was District Attorney Pat McCarran, a Democrat who later became a U.S. senator from Nevada.

Chapter 2

1. The school was founded to educate the children of Cal Tech faculty, and in the early years only went through the ninth grade. At present, it includes from kindergarten to the twelfth grade and is one of the most prestigious schools in Southern California in its annual crop of Merit Scholars. It and Harvard-Marymount in West Los Angeles are considered the two outstanding preparatory schools in Southern California based on academic results.

2. From April of 1942 to August 1945, CNAC crews flew more than 38,000 trips over the Hump, providing essential supplies and support to the Chinese and American forces in the CBI theater. The routes and terrain were dangerous, and several of the crews were lost in the operations.

3. During the war—tragically—many of these temples were ransacked and the artwork stolen or destroyed. In this and many other respects, the India that Frost encountered no longer exists.

4. He served with distinction and received numerous citations and decorations. After his return, he was debriefed by Army Intelligence and the Office of Strategic Services (OSS). He also became a lifetime member of the Hump Pilots Association, and still looks with considerable pride on his service during the war.

5. This notion has endured, and in 2009 reached the U.S. Supreme Court. The case involved the question of whether "business methods" in the financial sector are patentable. The Court held that the invention in the case before it could not be patented, but left open the possibility that other business methods might be patentable. Bilski *v.* Kappos (08-964) 2010 WL 255 192 (June 28, 2010).

Chapter 3

1. Bicknell began practicing law in California after he arrived from Wisconsin on a wagon train, following the Civil War.

Chapter 4

1. See Eli Wald, "The Rise and Fall of the WASP and Jewish Law Firms," 60 *Stanford Law Review* 1803 (2008).

2. A fuller discussion of the opening of the New York office and Frost's growth strategy appears in chapter 6.

Chapter 5

1. Hoffman and his wife, Dorothy Hoffman, owned a large estate in the Linda Vista area of Pasadena that overlooked the Arroyo Seco and the Rose Bowl. This estate was used by the Hoffmans during parts of the winter season, especially over the Christmas and New Year holidays. There, they entertained members of Congress, government officials, and prominent members of the private sector.

2. Frost and Cochran remained friends thereafter, and Cochran became the godmother of Frost's daughter, Polly.

3. Frost and the Hoffmans remain close friends to this day. Lathrop is Frost's daughter's godfather; Dorothy Anne was Frost's son's godmother until his son's recent death; and Frost is the godfather of Lathrop and Dorothy Anne's son Peter.

4. His background had been as one of the "Whiz Kids" at Ford Motor Company, immediately after World War II, along with Robert McNamara and a few others who had previously worked together at the Pentagon.

5. They were the trustees of the Chandler Trusts and the directors of Chandis Securities Company (Frost was later asked to join the board of Chandis). These two trusts, created in 1936, and Chandis together, held a super majority of the outstanding stock of Times Mirror. Chandis also owned, usually in joint ventures, a collection of land investments that had been put together by Harry Chandler in prior years.

6. Otis Chandler personally chose Tom Johnson to be his successor, according to Frost.

7. In due course, Dr. Franklin Murphy, then chancellor at UCLA, was asked to join the company as president and Norman Chandler became chairman.

8. Frost's influence on the Times Mirror Board was underscored by the distinguished speakers at a farewell dinner when Frost retired from the board.

Remarks by Dr. Franklin Murphy, Robert F. Erburu, Shelby Coffey, and Otis Chandler himself credited Frost with helping the company become one of the most preeminent media companies in the nation during Frost's tenure. Otis Chandler's remarks included the following observations and praise of Frost:

> Well, Dan and I go back a long way. I started in this company in 1947 and worked in the summers of 1947, '48 and '49; joined the company out of the air force as a full-time employee of The Times in 1953, so I'm coming up on forty years. I don't remember the first time I met you, Dan. I came into management in 1958 as a general manager of the now defunct *Mirror News,* and I think that you just about then became involved with the company—1958 or 1959, I think it was. Bob said 1959. I became a director in 1963 and Dan a director in 1967. But, Dan, Franklin has so eloquently said, I think has and without question in my mind, done more for the growth and development of this company and its various divisions than any outside director. I think of him as really almost an employee of the company because he has done so much for so many of us. And, Mia, if I may take the liberty tonight, I know if our father, Norman, were here—and he's probably here spiritually because he would love to be here, and my mother who is very alive and quite well and can't be here, she's going to be ninety-one in May and they were so devoted to you, Dan—I know that if Norman were up here, Bob, he would be saying what I am going to say, which is "Dan we thank you for everything you have done for Buff and myself and my son, Otis, and the company and the Chandler family through Chandis. You've been a marvelous supporter of what we believe in, what we stand for and God bless."
>
> So, to you, Dan, God bless.

9. Frost is enormously proud of the eagle sculpture that he received from the board when he retired from service in 1992.

10. Tejon Ranch is an important part of California history. Its headquarters is located about sixty miles south of Bakersfield, near a state park commemorating the headquarters of a U.S. Calvary Unit established before the

Civil War. This fort was abandoned when the regiment was sent east to fight in the Civil War.

11. During the period that Frost served as Tejon Ranch's legal counsel and as a director on its board—the 1960s through the 1980s—Tejon Ranch consisted of approximately 280,000 acres. The operating part of the ranch traversed the southern part of the San Joaquin Valley, extended east into a mountainous area, and north to a parcel just east of the city of Bakersfield, also containing miles of freeway frontage on both sides of Interstate 5. A minor oil and gas field on the property has been pumping for decades. Until 1999, the ranch also owned the largest cattle herd in California. Tejon's brand, the Cross and Crescent, is registered as brand 1 in the California registry of brands. It was copied from the brand used by the king of Spain for his royal cattle, and signified the joining of Christianity and the Muslim world in southern Spain following the defeat of the Moorish invasion centuries before.

Tejon always had a shortage of water for irrigation purposes until the advent of the California Water Project established under the regime of Governor Pat Brown. Substantial easements carry this water system to the end of the San Joaquin Valley and—by means of a famous, enormous pumping system—lifts it over the mountainous area and, by gravity flow, the water continues down to the Los Angeles basin.

Tejon was put together by General Beale, an early surveyor general in the Western Territories, at the end of the nineteenth century. Around 1900 it was bought by a consortium of several wealthy Southern California families (who had collaborated in many deals), including General M. H. Sherman, the Chandler family, and a few other friends.

12. After the war, Avery brought in Russ Smith to administer the company, since Avery felt it was imperative that he remain free to invent new products and oversee all technological development. He also brought onto the board Pete Peck, a partner of Latham & Watkins (counsel for the company) and Larry Tollenaere, the CEO of a successful, medium-sized industrial company.

13. When Avery's first wife died in 1964, the estate encountered significant difficulties due to the mishandling of estate-planning matters by a previous lawyer. The Price-Waterhouse firm, which then was performing auditing

services for Avery's businesses, recommended three lawyers be interviewed for the estate assignment. One of the three lawyers was Frost.

The mid-1960s were a period of conflict between the accounting and legal professions. Lawyers had become anxious about accountants assuming greater responsibility for client affairs and worried that accountants were beginning to practice law without a license. Frost did not oppose the accounting firms in this turf battle; rather, he maintained good relations with the major accounting firms in California and accepted their incursions into what some lawyers perceived as their terrain. Fittingly, accountants trusted Frost, which may have prompted them to make the important, even life-altering, referral of Frost to Avery. Another lesson thus can be drawn from Frost's representation of Avery: benefits result more often from forging alliances in business matters and softening the edges of one's disagreements than by cultivating animosity or protecting turf unconditionally. Frost had an instinct for such appeasement, and he knew when to tuck in his competitive instincts in order to maintain relationships, rather than draw a line in the sand for the sake of principles, pride, or position.

14. Frost served on the board for thirty years.

15. Frost also encouraged others to follow the Avery model. He advised his young scholarship recipients, for example, to leverage their educational opportunities and reach beyond their immediate communities, families, and tribes. See chapter 7. Rather than returning to their local communities to tend to others one-on-one as doctors, lawyers, or other educated professionals in small-town contexts, Frost urged them to consider posts and opportunities in larger settings, in order to gain sufficient influence and wealth to make a more substantial, systemic community impact. This advice, of course, not only was based on Frost's experience with Stan Avery, but also on his own life. Had Frost stayed in small-firm practice in Pasadena, rather than making the bolder move to Los Angeles and embracing big-firm practice, he likely could not have made the connections, or amassed the fortune that he later shared with various worthy causes.

16. Among Frost's favorites were the following:

External pressures unite; internal pressures divide.

Socialism leads to planned shortages.

You're always down on what you're not up on.

If you have the power, you don't have to use it.

On gravity: Nothing ever falls up.

On success: Always fail forward.

If there is money, it will be spent.

When you stop making mistakes, you are in deep trouble.

When the going gets rough, you get the best traction.

Try not to think the worst of anyone. The best is not that good.

Old age can kill you.

Nobody ever told me old age would be painful even when you're not sick.

If you walk to the other side of the room and then can't remember why, don't worry, it's exercise.

It is possible to be brilliant to the point of stupidity.

You have to hit bottom before you can bounce back.

Don't borrow money thinking it will solve all your problems. It only makes it possible to work on bigger ones.

If you are surrounded by cannibals, hospitality does not require that they be fed.

My unselfishness over the years has served me well.

It's easy to grow old but hard to stay young.

Always prepare for the best. The worst isn't going to happen either.

Acquisition of property is fun. Disposing of it can be painful and costly.

The only thing worse than a bad government is no government.

It's funny. A man spends the first half of his life trying to kill himself and the last half trying to stay alive.

As a generality, individuals tend to work together; organizations do not. Even divisions within a company prefer to be self-sufficient.

Never cut people down. They will just cut you up.

If you swim with the tide, you'll go too fast. If you swim against the tide, you'll go too slow. Float!

I don't like to go to funerals. I don't even want to go to my own.

17. Here again, Frost's good relations with the accounting firms was an important basis for the referral.

18. Parsons had been one of the co-contractors for Boulder Dam and a good friend and business rival of Steve Bechtel and Henry Kaiser, who were also involved in construction of the dam.

19. The use of the *Argo*, and its treatment for Internal Revenue Code purposes, was another issue in the tax dispute inherited by Frost and Price Waterhouse.

20. Because the emperor was a member of the Coptic Catholic Church and dated his ancestry back to King Solomon and the Queen of Sheba, he was thus much revered as a true descendant of these biblical figures. Much of the Ethiopian folk art of the time depicts the biblical union that gave rise to the emperor's ancient family ties to some of the oldest written records of Christianity.

21. The geologic discovery work on the concession proved to be very successful as a mining project. However, the venture had to be later terminated for technical reasons because the excavation for the mine had ended up too close to the Red Sea, and serious seepage started to flood the mining operation.

As it turned out, the concession would have had to have been terminated in any event because of a revolution within Ethiopia that overthrew the emperor and his government. The emperor and his immediate family perished during the aftermath, as did many of his cabinet members (some of whom had been aboard the *Argo*).

In this regard, an unusual experience occurred in the mid-1990s, when Frost and his wife hailed a taxi in downtown Seattle to go to a meeting at the Port of Seattle. Frost immediately knew the driver was from Ethiopia. He asked him what part of Ethiopia he came from. The driver was surprised that Frost had identified his nationality, and said he was a refugee from Addis after the takeover by the Communist insurgent forces. He said he had been in the emperor's cabinet and had been able to escape from Addis into the countryside during the days of terror following the collapse of the kingdom. He then had made his way out of the country and eventually to the United States through underground sources loyal to the king. He mentioned that there was a fairly large Ethiopian community in Seattle. Frost invited him to have breakfast with him the following morning. During that meeting Frost learned a great deal about what had happened to the emperor, his family, and members of the government. The cab driver also showed Frost many pictures of his family, his career, and his tribulations in Ethiopia.

22. The New York architectural firm of Skidmore Owens had been employed to design the airport building (constructed by Parsons) covering an enormous area to house pilgrims flying in from all over the world, particularly Africa, to visit Mecca at the time of the Hajj. The Skidmore firm designed the airport building like a Bedouin tent. This architectural design won enormous worldwide recognition and many international awards. From a long distance away, flying into Jeddah one can see this giant airport building. Frost recalls that it appeared to be floating in the air without visible support of any kind.

23. The first was in the Ventura-Santa Barbara area, leading to the formation of the Union Oil Company.

24. "B" Kleberg Johnson's parents died when he was young, and he was raised at King Ranch headquarters by the famous "Uncle Bob" Kleberg. King Ranch was, and is, an enormous landholding in southern Texas (then reputedly the largest privately owned contiguous landholding in the United States, encompassing approximately 800,000 acres, with additional acreage nearby). Its original headquarters, built before the Civil War, was a historic hacienda-style, thickly walled, large building. Today it is used for large-scale entertaining, particularly during the famous King Ranch quarter horse and cattle auctions. The main room is two stories high; the second floor consists of numerous guestrooms connected by a corridor that extends entirely around that floor above the main room. Along this walkway are pictures involving Kleberg family history, going back some 150 years. Of particular interest to Frost, when he was a guest there, were Civil War–era pictures of the Kleberg women in riding clothes, bearing rifles. At that time most of their men were

away from the ranch fighting in the Confederate Army. These Kleberg women and their foremen and ranch hands defended the ranch against invasions from Mexico and domestic bandits.

The walls of the old headquarters still show the effects of rifle and small cannon fire. The nearest town to the King headquarters is Alice, Texas, named after Uncle Bob Kleberg's mother, Alice King.

Frost also recalls attending an auction of Santa Gertrudis bulls with "Uncle Bob Kleberg" of Texas's King Ranch, where Frost almost bought a 1,500-pound animal inadvertently when he put his hand to his right ear and the auctioneer mistook the gesture for a bid; fortunately, another bidder raised the ante, and Frost slowly exhaled.

25. Frost credits Dr. Bing with a medical intervention that proved to be profoundly important to Frost's health and that sealed their friendship. Frost had been diagnosed with serious melanoma and, due to a faulty initial pathology analysis, was scheduled for radical surgery on his face. Dr. Bing immediately scheduled Frost for a reevaluation by the top surgical oncologist at UCLA, who found the error in the original analysis and determined that the melanoma was far less deep than previously believed. A successful, far more modern surgical procedure removed all of the melanoma, and Frost recovered completely. He and Bing have remained friends ever since.

Chapter 6

1. The office was a small one, but held its own, according to Frost. Robert Gelber, Ronald Beard, and John Cochran headed up the office during those years, and Frost credits Beard in particular with assuring that he office succeeded.

Frost also describes his "eye-opening" experience in negotiating an acquisition in France for the firm's client Purex. Frost describes the experience as follows:

"Purex desired to acquire a leading French soap company. Since I had been on their acquisition team in the U.S., they wanted me to do the same in France. It was their first overseas endeavor. During these negotiations I learned that centuries of history of revolutions and monarchies plus two world wars had formed the French business character into something quite different from their U.S. counterparts, who had so much regulatory control. I learned that the French companies kept at least three sets of books, one for the public authorities, a second for the public shareholders, and the third for the few who really needed to know the truth. Gaining access to that third set of books was almost impossible. The French were experts at currency exchange and across-border cash transactions and hidden deposits. Obviously that was about the only way that wealthy families were able to survive the turmoil and retain their wealth."

2. Barker was succeeded by Ronald Beard in 1991. Beard was succeeded by Wesley Howell Jr. in 1997. Ken Doran assumed the managing partner post in 2002 and still holds the position as of this writing.

3. The full texts of his most significant speeches appear as appendices to this volume.

4. Charles Rappleye, "Palace Coup," *LA Weekly*, September 3–September 9, 1993, 18, quote on 20 (quoting an unnamed Gibson, Dunn & Crutcher partner).

5. Gay Jervey, "Mission Accomplished," *American Lawyer*, September 1986, 80, quote on 82.

6. Kim Masters, "Orchestra Seeks New Maestro," *Legal Times*, December 23/30, 1985, 28.

7. Frost was responsible for the firm's acquisition of American Airlines as a client. While Frost was on the Times Mirror Board, he became close friends with Al Casey, then executive vice president of Times Mirror. Later, Casey left Times Mirror and became CEO of the holding company for American Airlines. One day, when Frost was at a Tejon Ranch board meeting at the ranch headquarters, he received an emergency call from Casey calling on behalf of American Airlines. Although Casey was CEO of the holding company, Bob Crandall was the president of American Airlines itself, a subsidiary of the holding company. Frost remembers the anxiety in Casey's voice as Casey informed him that Crandall had had an indiscreet telephone conversation with the head of Braniff Airlines. The conversation was taped, and the tape had found its way into the hands of the Justice Department. Casey said that Crandall and American Airlines were being investigated by the Justice Department and asked for Frost's assistance. Within a few hours a Gibson Dunn antitrust partner, Bob Cooper, was in Dallas. In due course, Cooper

worked out a favorable settlement of the matter. This representation led to other legal business from American Airlines for Gibson Dunn. American Airlines became a major client.

8. See Tamar Lewin, "Growth of a Coast Law Firm," *New York Times*, March 14, 1982, Business Section, B-1; Steven Brill, "LA's Management Moguls," *American Lawyer*, March 1982, 6; James S. Granelli, "Gibson Dunn's Global Growth," *National Law Journal* 4, no. 24 (February 22, 1982): 1.

9. William Overend, "NY Challenge: Legal Boom Ends Calm at LA Firms," *Los Angeles Times*, September 27, 1987, pt. 1, p. 1, col. 1.

10. Gay Jervey, "Mission Accomplished," *American Lawyer*, September 1986, 80, quote on 81.

11. Malcolm Gladwell, *The Tipping Point: How Little Things Can Make a Big Difference* (Boston: Little, Brown, 2000).

12. Kim Masters, "Orchestra Seeks New Maestro," *Legal Times*, December 23/30, 1985, p.1.

13. Ibid.

Chapter 7

1. The service was held at San Miguel Mission, a place with great historical significance for the Blackburn-Frost family.

2. In recounting the trip, his father again summoned his most eloquent voice and described the scene as follows:

> Clear blue skies, a bright sun, clear beautiful water, a slight breeze and a temperature of about 70 degrees.
>
> All the passengers gathered on the foredeck where there was a long padded bench and a spacious room for the proceedings. Karin Frost was sitting on the bench on the far port side. Elisa (her daughter) was in front of her. Karin then opened the urn and the two bags of ashes were carefully extracted. Elisa then took the tie off of one of the bags and went to the rail, leaned over, and poured the ashes into the sea. The sea was very calm and the ashes formed a still cloud beside the boat, the cloud drifting slightly away. She then untied and deposited the second bag and poured the ashes from it near the first cloud of ashes. At that time, it seemed that the water directly below

became almost turbulent. The two separate clouds of ashes seemed to swirl together and, at the same time, moved off the side of the boat as one. One passenger observed that it was like a cage of tightly confined birds finally being set free. The captain's mate, observing from the bridge, later made a similar statement and added that the ashes also took on an iridescent quality while swirling together.

Suddenly, seemingly out of nowhere, three dolphins appeared, circled the ashes and the boat, leaping far out of the water, sometimes in unison and sometimes individually. This went on for approximately fifteen minutes before the captain turned the boat towards the east and headed back to the harbor. The dolphins followed the boat for probably another thirty minutes. The dolphins repeatedly "led" the boat, at times traveling slightly underwater and then jumping clear of the water, very close to and in front of the bow, and under the boat, crossing back and forth. Elisa Daus laid down on the bow sprit and watched.

Karin Frost turned to [Frost], who was sitting next to her and said, "Is this a sign?" [Frost] replied, "Karin, it is a miraculous sign from [Dr. Frost] that he is free, he is happy and that he is swimming with the dolphins."

Chapter 8

1. See Alex Williams, "No Longer Their Golden Ticket," *New York Times*, January 17, 2010, Style Section, p. 1 (discussing the "depreciating value" of the associate post in elite corporate law firms).

178–82(figs.); issues for, 157–60; leadership of, 82–84, 98–101, 122–23, 174–75; long-term planning, 142–45; Management Committee, x, 81, 155–56; management of, xii, 79–81, 101–2, 140–42, 147–48, 149–50, 175–76; overseas expansion of, 45–46, 77; professional changes in, 43–44; profitability of, 86–89, 136–37, 165–67; size of, 73–74; Sturdy's management of, 74–78; succession and retirement plan, 78–79; Times Mirror, 54–59; vision for, 98–99; western character of, 84–86, 103, 104, 134–35, 148–49, 156–57

Gladwell, Malcolm: *The Tipping Point,* 97–98

Goa, Father, 114

Godbold, Woody, 157

Godshaux, Lazarus, 8

Great Depression: impacts of, 10–11

Great Recession, 121

Greenbaum Wolf, 153

Green Giant foods, 107

Griffiths, Bill, 53

Guilin (Kweilin), 24

Gutierrez-Morfin, Yvette, 112

HAAP. *See* Hispanic Academic Achievement Program

Haile Selassie, 67, 211n.20

Haiphong, 24

Hanoi: French First Army in, 24

Harkness, Barbara Rickey Frost, 10

Haskell, Arnold, 59, 60

Haskell, Don, 108; as client and friend, 59, 60, 61

Haskins, Sam, 141

Head School, 6

health: and climate, 15–16, 18

Helms, Paul, 52

Hereford (Texas): cattle-feeding and financing business in, 108, 203n.1

Hispanic Academic Achievement Program (HAAP), 110–12

Hispanics: in eastern Washington, 110

Hoffman, Lathrop, 51, 53, 206n.3

Hoffman, Paul G., 51, 52, 53, 206n.1

Hoffman Company Board, Paul G., 53

Hoffman family, 206nn.1, 3; as clients, 51–53

homesteading: in Carson Valley, 5

Honda Motor Company, 70

Hong Kong, 155

Hufford, Harry, 161

Hump, the, *photo album*; supplying China over, 22, 23, 205n.2

identity: collective, 98–99

Imperial War Museum (Duxford, UK): Kohima Memorial, *photo album*

Imphal, battle of, 21

India, 23, 205n.3; Bose's Army, 20–21; medical transport service in, 21–22

Indian independence movement, 21

Inheritance Tax Division, 36

Internal Revenue Service (IRS), 36, 66, 70–71

investments: Crocker Center as, 1 66–67; Frost's business, 105–8; Frost's philanthropic, 109–15

irrigation: Nevada, 6; Tejon Ranch, 61, 208n.11

Japan: Gibson Dunn offices in, 155

Japanese army: Bose's Army in, 20–21

Jedda: airport at, 67, 212n.22

Jenner& Block, 168

Johnson, Belton (B) Kleberg, 70, 212n.24

Johnson, Omar, 54

Johnson, Pitch, 154

Johnson, Tom, 56, 57, 206n.6

Kadison, Pfaelzer, Woodard, Quinn & Rossi, 45